WHO
COULD
EVER
LOVE YOU

WHO COULD COULD EVER LOVE YOU

A Family Memoir

MARY L. TRUMP

ST. MARTIN'S PRESS
NEW YORK

First published in the United States by St. Martin's Press, an imprint of
St. Martin's Publishing Group

www.stmartins.com

The Library of Congress Cataloging-in-Publication Data is available upon
request.

ISBN 978-1-250-27847-0 (hardcover)
ISBN 978-1-250-27848-7 (ebook)

Our books may be purchased in bulk for promotional, educational, or business
use. Please contact your local bookseller or the Macmillan Corporate and
Premium Sales Department at 1-800-221-7945, extension 5442, or by email at
MacmillanSpecialMarkets@macmillan.com.

First Edition: 2024

10 9 8 7 6 5 4 3 2 1

To Avary
and
E. Jean

When I consider the brief span of my life absorbed into the eternity which precedes and will succeed it . . . the small space I occupy and which I see swallowed up in the infinite immensity of spaces of which I know nothing and which know nothing of me, I take fright and am amazed to see myself here rather than there: there is no reason for me to be here rather than there, now rather than then.

—BLAISE PASCAL, *Pensées*

AUTHOR'S NOTE

This is a true story, though some names and details have been changed.

CONTENTS

PROLOGUE

2021

I exhaled as the needle slid into my veins. Ketamine flowing through my body felt like an act of desperation—it *was* an act of desperation.

Four years earlier, in 2017, I had checked myself into a facility in Tucson, Arizona, for intensive trauma treatment. Now I was in trouble again, experiencing some of the same symptoms that had landed me there—dissociation, an inability to concentrate, and increasing social isolation. It was getting harder to leave my apartment, let alone get off the couch. Which was weird, because by then I was a public person. People saw me on television several times a week. A year earlier, I'd published a book that had launched me into the national conversation about my uncle Donald. Everybody was a shut-in during the pandemic, so no one noticed that I was, too. The problem was, by 2021 everyone else was going outside again, and I wasn't.

Within five minutes of the ketamine entering my bloodstream, the world had expanded and I began to fall through it slowly and pleasantly. I felt lighter than I had in a very long time, almost euphoric. Anything seemed possible. I made connections in my mind, I made plans, I saw potential.

I suddenly had an overwhelming desire to text. I started with close friends, then people I thought were my friends but who turned out not to be. Then I texted people I didn't know particularly well but with whom I still felt it was crucially important for me to share the fact that I was high. "I am so high."

And then I saw the coat hook.

I'd recently read Mike Sowden's *Everything Is Amazing* Substack newsletter about pareidolia, the human impulse to construct visual patterns that aren't really there. This led me to a Reddit post on the phenomenon that featured a picture of a metal coat hook under which had been written in Sharpie, "Drunk octopus wants to fight you." And there it was, exactly the kind of oval, two-armed coat hook that is screwed to doors in doctors' offices all over the world. I needed to share this, too.

Because of the needle in my left arm, only my right hand was free, so it took a while to focus the camera on my phone and get a photograph that wasn't too blurry. I proceeded to text it to all the same people, noting that it was one of the funniest things I'd ever seen.

Slowly, though, things began to shift. I still felt light, almost invincible, but my vision was clearing and everything was beginning to feel more solid.

An hour had passed. The nurse came in to remove the needle and check my vitals. It would be another thirty minutes before I felt steady enough to go home. It was during that space that a thought came to me as if carved in glass, so clear, so stark was it: *I don't want to die.*

I texted that to everybody, too.

I had met with the psychiatrist who ran the ketamine clinic, a mild man in his mid-seventies who seemed beyond surprise, only once. Before we discussed the treatment—how it worked and what I might expect—the doctor needed to find out whether I was a good candidate. I needed his reassurance that there wouldn't be any side effects I wasn't willing to risk. The only drug I'd ever tried was pot, a handful of times, in college. I'd found being high unpleasant and, at least once, terrifying, and I wanted to make sure this experience would be different.

I'd always liked that part—the intake, the initial gathering of information, the telling of the story. Over the decades, my family's history, and my own, had become simply that—a story I told to therapists and psychiatrists whenever I decided to start therapy again. I'd become so detached from the narrative I spun that I no longer had any feelings about it, which afforded me a certain pleasure of mastery—over the material, over my ability to describe the contours of my pathologies as if from a great remove, over myself. The narrative I'd constructed to explain who I was—to explain how I had arrived at a particular moment—remained neatly contained within the borders I'd erected long ago.

In December 2021, though, it was no longer that simple and had long since stopped being true. There was a new part of the story I couldn't control because, although it had a massive impact on my life on an almost day-to-day basis, it fundamentally had nothing to do with me: having to sit in front of a total stranger and say, "I'm here because five years ago, I lost control of my life. I'm here because the world has fallen away and I don't know how to find my way back. I'm here because Donald Trump is my uncle."

Saying it filled me with a shame that proved impossible to detach myself from. Hearing those words come out of my mouth unsettled me; they needed saying, but felt like a curse. And whether they had any explanatory power depended almost entirely on the perspective of whoever was listening.

Saying it reminded me of all the times, at a restaurant or a store, that I'd used a credit card and was asked, "Are you related?" I always said, "No." And the response was always some version of "Don't you wish you were?"

When I finally confessed, the doctor raised his eyebrows and sighed. "I'm sorry," he said. "That must be very difficult for you."

I shrugged. I didn't know where to start.

One of the most disturbing things I learned during my weeks in treatment was that, for the better part of my adult life, I had been merely subsisting. I recognized the truth of this as soon as it was presented to me. Initially, I reacted with resentment. What's the point of recognizing you're at the bottom of a deep hole that other people have put you in if you don't have any of the equipment necessary to climb out?

But it's better to know. It's always better to know. I'm still figuring out what to do with the knowledge.

To that end, at the Tucson facility, I had to do a lot of writing outside of individual therapy and groups. In one exercise I was asked to list six reasons I wanted to stay in treatment. For number six I wrote:

"I want to live."

As of autumn 2023, my life has gotten smaller. Days go by without my seeing another human being. Sometimes I can't remember the last time I went outside.

Yesterday, I brought the grocery delivery in from the hallway. The handles of the bags were cool to the touch and the bags themselves carried the scent of late autumn with hints of winter. That surprised me, to find I've missed another season. I've missed so many things—another holiday, another trip, more moments to connect than I can count.

I started writing this book because I realized I was killing myself—with stress, with self-loathing, but above all with isolation that started on November 9, 2016. But I don't want to die. I want to live.

PART I

The Dark Beauty of Recall

You know what I'd do if I were King? She never was a queen or a fairy she was always a king or a giant or a general.

—WILLIAM FAULKNER,
The Sound and the Fury

1

1969

The lights spread out below my window, keeping me tethered. I found them beautiful, sparkling to dispel any possibility of total darkness, glittering on the other side of the dividing line that ran through my neighborhood. Jamaica, where I lived with my mother, Linda, and brother, Fred C. Trump III (whom we called Fritz), was on the wrong side of the tracks from Jamaica Estates, the white, upper-middle-class neighborhood where my grandparents lived and my father, Fred Trump Jr., and his siblings, Maryanne, Elizabeth, Donald, and Robert, had grown up.

But even Jamaica was segregated. My apartment building, the Highlander, stood at the top of the hill that formed the southern border of the part of town called Jamaica Hills (although I had no idea that's what it was called). This part of the neighborhood, almost exclusively white, with its tree-lined streets and a park with towering oaks and a pond that reached all the way back toward Jamaica High School, felt almost suburban, at least to a kid who didn't know what a suburb was. It stood in stark contrast to South Jamaica, which was predominately Black and urban.

My bed was almost flush against a wall with south-facing windows. We were only a few miles from John F. Kennedy International Airport, and large commercial planes flew past my window every few minutes. Not long before, my father, Freddy, a pilot for TWA, had sat in the cockpit of 707s, taking off on his way to places I hadn't yet heard of. But I wouldn't know any of that for decades. In 1969, I was four years old.

Diagonally across from where my head lay on the pillow, the moon rose every night. Its light tethered me, too; its steady presence helped me keep time. It kept me company on those nights when I couldn't sleep, which, after Dad left for good, was often.

It had become easier for us since Dad moved back in with his parents, to the place we called the House. The tension in our own home faded. I no longer had to dodge the fights that often sparked between him and my mother—because of his drinking, mostly, but also because her anger about it caused them both to be cruel. Instead, I'd begun to learn how to walk on the eggshells of my mother's quiet despair.

They had both fallen so far from the early, heady days of their relationship, when my father was about to take his place at Trump Management as his father's right-hand man, and they spent evenings in the city with friends at the hottest clubs and weekends flying to Montauk or Bimini in Dad's Piper Cherokee. By 1967, my father's career and health had deteriorated; my mother was effectively trapped with two very young children in a run-down apartment that we rented from my grandfather and that she hated; and their marriage had disintegrated so thoroughly that it was almost impossible to imagine how these two wholly unsuited people had come together in the first place. My mother once told me that Freddy Trump was the most handsome man she'd ever met, and he could make her laugh. At twenty-two, that might have seemed enough. What my father saw in her was harder to discern, but she was pretty and admiring. Perhaps at twenty-three that was enough for him.

Now, seven years later, nearly thirty years old, my mother had no money beyond whatever was given to her for basic expenses and had no resources with which to make a new start. On top of this, her struggles with depression and her own futility were made worse by her inability to locate the reasons her life had unraveled so precipitously.

2

My mother, Linda, grew up in Kalamazoo, Michigan, in the 1940s.

Her father, Mike Clapp, was in some ways a working-class version of her future father-in-law, Fred Trump Sr.—entrepreneurial and hardworking, unaffectionate but a good provider, strict and accustomed to getting his own way. He had another side to him, too—like Freddy, his future son-in-law, he wanted to be a pilot. Mike started taking flying lessons right out of high school, but the Depression—and his father, Willis Clapp—had put a stop to his dreams.

Willis had suffered a serious head wound when Mike was still a young boy. Often in pain and unable to work, he spent most of his days sitting by the window staring into space. Usually taciturn, Willis had a frightening temper, and it was impossible to know what triggered it, making it difficult—and dangerous—for Mike's mother, Nellie, to be alone with her husband.

Nellie, a spitfire who drove a car at a time when few women did, had borne the burden of supporting the family since her husband's injury. She took in laundry, which back in the 1920s was backbreaking work. Clothes and linens had to be washed by hand in large buckets using a washboard, hung on a line to dry, and then pressed with a heavy flatiron heated on the stove.

Even so, every evening after work, Nellie took a bath, fixed her hair, and changed into one of the colorful cotton dresses she'd sewn by hand before starting dinner.

Linda's mother, Mary Rolfe, had left home after her own mother died, because her father quickly remarried and she and her new stepmother didn't get along. Mary moved from Menominee, Michigan, to Kalamazoo in the early 1920s to live with her aunt Pearl. She got a job at the YWCA, where she met Mike Clapp at one of the Y's Saturday night dances. They married in 1933. Their first daughter, Carol, was born a year later, and Linda was born in 1939.

Mike, who owned a fairly successful feed mill, was exempt from serving in World War II because of his young family. In the early 1940s he sold the mill so he and his brother-in-law could buy a semitruck in order to provide long-distance delivery service. Mike loved the work, but it meant being away from home a lot, often for long stretches, while Mary and Carol were left to take care of the household. Mary also volunteered for the Red Cross to support the war effort. Around this time, she began experiencing extreme joint pain and fatigue. Her doctors diagnosed her with rheumatoid arthritis, and by 1949, she was sometimes in so much pain she couldn't get out of bed.

Cortisone and gold shots were prescribed to relieve the pain, but not much was known about arthritis at that time, and the medications didn't work consistently. Mary's condition worsened rapidly—the harsh winters in Michigan were becoming increasingly difficult for her to bear—and her doctors recommended the family move to Florida. They'd vacationed in Florida before and liked it, but nobody, especially Linda, wanted to leave Kalamazoo. In August 1952, however, shortly after Linda turned thirteen, Mike packed his truck with all of their belongings and drove the family to Fort Lauderdale.

The Clapps stayed in an efficiency apartment at a hotel by the beach for a couple of weeks while they looked for a house. Mike sold his truck and used the proceeds to buy the restaurant— more of a clam shack, really—next door to the hotel. He knew nothing about the restaurant business, but it had once been a popular takeout place and the location was good, so he thought that, with the help of his wife and children, he could make it work.

Mike and Mary were an affectionate couple, and Mike clearly loved her, but he controlled pretty much everything and she had little or no say in any family decisions. As soon as Mary got sick, though, she became the entire focus of her husband's life, to the detriment of his relationships with his daughters. It's not that he didn't care about them, or that he was actively cruel, but his wife came first and there wasn't much attention left over for them.

For Linda, the first year in Florida was long and lonely. The junior high school she attended, in the barracks of a former naval air station, was a stark comedown from the beautiful, newly built school she'd attended in Kalamazoo. She made some friends freshman year, but her father made her work at the restaurant after school and on weekends, so she didn't have much of a social life. Her job included taking orders and peeling shrimp. She hated it. Since the move to Florida, Linda had become painfully shy, and during her breaks, she sat on a stool in the back doing homework, which she preferred to waiting on customers, some of whom, especially on weekends, were kids from the high school. She couldn't bear the thought of being seen by them. In fact, she hated everything having to do with the restaurant.

Back in Kalamazoo, Linda had had friends, a community, and an environment that compensated her for what she wasn't getting from her parents. There was nothing compensatory about Fort Lauderdale until she joined the synchronized swimming team her sophomore year. Over the next three years the camaraderie with her teammates made life in high school manageable. The team performed all over South Florida and competed in statewide competitions. When Linda wasn't in the pool, she swam along the shoreline of the Atlantic Ocean to increase her endurance. I used to picture her slicing through the water with her powerful, confident strokes, the waves silvering as they crested, the sun reflecting off the schools of mullet keeping pace.

3

In August 1958, Freddy Trump rented a plane from an airfield in Bethlehem, Pennsylvania, and flew with his best friend, Billy Drake, down to Nassau in the Bahamas for a short getaway before the fall semester at Lehigh University started. It was there, one evening at the poolside bar, that Freddy met a pretty, petite blonde named Linda Clapp.

Linda and her friend Harriet had just flown into Nassau from Florida for vacation. At nineteen, she had never met anyone like Freddy Trump. Dressed in black slacks, white shirt, skinny black tie, and madras jacket, he was, at twenty, different from every boy Linda had ever known. Freddy was six feet tall but slender, never weighing more than 152 pounds. He was funny and talkative. He told Linda about the new Corvette he'd bought with money he'd earned working at the Chevy dealership near Lehigh, where he was a rising junior. He was very proud of his first car, but while he was in Nassau, his older sister, Maryanne, called to tell him she'd somehow managed to get his Corvette crushed in a car elevator. Freddy didn't take it too hard—he wasn't that kind of guy.

Before Harriet and Linda left to go back to Florida, they told the boys they were planning a trip to New York the following summer. Freddy and Billy offered to show them around the city, and Freddy handed Linda a slip of paper with his name and phone number. "Call as soon as you land," he said. And then he smiled at her.

Although the streets of New York in the summer of 1959 were not filled with people singing and dancing, as Linda half expected after all the movies she'd seen, there were town houses and skyscrapers and little restaurants a few steps down from the sidewalk. She did call Freddy a day or two after she and Harriet arrived, and he and Billy took them out a few times for dinner and drinks and shows in the city. They also spent a day at Billy's summer place in Southampton, where Freddy had first learned to love being out on the water. On the way, they stopped at the House briefly to switch cars. There, Linda met thirteen-year-old Donald, who was two months away from being shipped off to a military academy, and Freddy's mother, who glanced disapprovingly at Linda's capris but didn't have much to say.

The four of them enjoyed a wonderful few days together. Harriet was already engaged, and Billy had a girlfriend in Jamaica Estates, but Linda and Freddy clearly had something between them. Freddy offered to take Linda out for a final dinner, just the two of them, the night before she and Harriet returned to Florida. But he never called. When Linda didn't hear from him, she called the House.

"Hello?" It was Donald.

"This is Linda, Freddy's friend. We met a few days ago. May I speak with him?"

"He's not here. He went bear hunting," Donald said, then hung up.

Linda had known Freddy only briefly, but he'd spoken to her about his love of animals, and how much he wished he could have had a pet growing up. She couldn't imagine him trying to kill an animal for sport. She sensed a lie, but whose lie was it? She only knew that her attraction to Freddy had grown and she'd begun to have feelings toward him. Now he'd ditched her. On the way back to Florida, Harriet did most of the driving because Linda cried halfway down the Eastern Seaboard.

4

Once back in Fort Lauderdale, Linda considered her options. Despite receiving a small scholarship from Florida State University, she never seriously contemplated going to college, and her parents had no expectations either way.

She worked for a finance company right out of high school, but the entire business seemed to be based on tricking their mostly Black customers into taking loans with high interest rates despite the agents' making them sound reasonable.

After less than a year, she applied for a job at the phone company and became a long-distance operator—this was before direct dialing, so all calls had to be placed through an operator. It was considered lowly work at the time, but there weren't a lot of job opportunities for women in 1958 and she needed to make a living.

Finally, she applied for a position as a stewardess—something she'd always considered doing—with Mackey Airlines, a local outfit that made daily flights from Fort Lauderdale to the Bahamas. Linda had no intention of staying in Florida, and she thought working for an airline would be a good way to escape. She was up for a job as a customer service representative at the phone company—a position she hoped would give her more money and more confidence—but before her second interview, Mackey hired her. There was no turning back.

Linda started with the airline in February 1960 and flew to the Bahamas every day. The crew spent afternoons at the British Colonial, the same hotel where she'd met Freddy two years earlier, before flying back to Fort Lauderdale. When Linda turned twenty-one, she was accepted into the September class at National Airlines, a much bigger company that had routes all over the country. The new stewardesses were given a choice of three cities to be based in: Miami, Jacksonville, or New York. Linda picked New York.

The airline housed her and six of her fellow classmates at the Belmont Plaza Hotel, on Lexington Avenue in Manhattan, for a couple of weeks so they could look for a more permanent place to live. They settled on a two-bedroom apartment in Woodside, Queens, in a brand-new building on a tree-lined street. Although the apartment was small, they were never all there at the same time because of their schedules, so it made sense—and each one's share of the rent was manageable.

As much as they liked the neighborhood, however, they knew nothing about New York City geography. Queens, one of the five boroughs, is enormous. Although Woodside was close to LaGuardia, the other major New York area airport, it was far from Idlewild, as JFK was then called, especially if you had to take public transportation. In addition, there was no phone in the apartment; phone companies were reluctant to install them for airline employees because they moved around so often.

Schedules changed frequently, so the stewardesses had to wake up early and call the airline from the corner pay phone to find out if they were flying that day. If they were, they ran back to the apartment to get ready for work, then left for the lengthy commute: the elevated train from Woodside to Jackson Heights; the subway to Kew Gardens; and then the bus to the airport in Jamaica. The trip took almost an hour and a half each way—assuming everything went smoothly.

The roommates, realizing the logistics were untenable, decided to split into pairs and go their separate ways. Linda, who planned to room with her friend Jacquie, remembered that Freddy had mentioned his father owned a couple of apartment buildings in Queens. She still had his phone number, so she called him, and they arranged to meet to see if he could help her find a place to live.

Freddy was pleased to hear from her, even though they hadn't seen each other since the "bear hunting" incident almost two years earlier, and he offered to take her out for dinner. He picked up Linda in his new black Corvette, a replacement for the one Maryanne destroyed in the car elevator, and took her to a nice restaurant in the city. It was as if no time had passed. The next day, he met Linda and Jacquie in Jamaica, where Fred owned several buildings, to look at apartments.

Jamaica, only a fifteen-minute bus ride from Idlewild, was ideally located, but the rent for a one-bedroom at the Highlander, the first building they looked at, was $150 a month, much more than they could afford. The Saxony, a block away on the other side of Highland Avenue and right next to the nine-acre Captain Tilly Park, had a studio available for $110 a month, and they decided to move in right away. After paying first and last months' rent, Linda and Jacquie had very little money left over, so Freddy, already working at his father's company in Brooklyn, offered to buy some furniture to get them started. They agreed to pay him back when they could.

Freddy and Linda picked up where they left off. A ridiculously attractive couple, they spent evenings in the city with his friends from Sigma Alpha Mu, the fraternity he belonged to at Lehigh, and the National Guard, going to restaurants and shows at the Copacabana on East Sixtieth Street. When the summer rolled around, she and Freddy spent their weekends out east on Long Island with Billy and his girlfriend, Annamaria. Sometimes Freddy, who had learned how to fly while he was at Lehigh and had earned both his private and professional licenses by the time he graduated, rented a seaplane and flew them out to Billy's summer house, where they went water-skiing on Peconic Bay, or to Bimini in the Bahamas for a couple of days. Or they'd take Freddy's new boat, a mahogany Chris-Craft inboard he bought right after coming home from college, out on the Atlantic to Montauk, on the eastern tip of Long Island. Whenever he took off from Idlewild, he flew over the Rockaway, Queens, beach house of his fraternity brother Stu and tipped his wings.

By the summer of 1961, Linda and Freddy were engaged.

Their engagement lasted five months. Per tradition, the bride's family was expected to pay for the wedding, but because of her mother's medical expenses and her father's modest means, that responsibility fell to Linda. A New York wedding would be far too expensive, and Mary Clapp was now confined to a wheelchair, so a trip to New York would have been very hard on her. To solve both problems, they agreed it made sense to marry in Florida. Freddy's parents weren't pleased with the decision, but they didn't offer to help financially, either, and threw a New York reception when the newlyweds returned from their honeymoon.

The couple flew down to Fort Lauderdale once before the wedding so Freddy could meet his future in-laws. Linda's maternal grandfather, Claude Rolfe, happened to be visiting at the time, and he told his granddaughter that he didn't think Freddy was a good match for her. Her mother, on the other hand, adored him; her father was immediately enamored of the fact that his future son-in-law was a pilot; and Linda, of course, was in love. Nothing would change her mind.

The Trumps strongly hinted that the wedding invitations needed to be ordered from Tiffany's. Linda couldn't afford them, so Freddy helped her cover the expense. Her future sister-in-law Maryanne insisted they place a wedding announcement in *The*

New York Times and offered to help her write it, going so far as to suggest she claim to be taking classes at Columbia in the fall of that year—even though that wasn't true—because it wouldn't look good if Linda described herself as a "mere" high school graduate and stewardess. Maryanne also vetoed Freddy's plan to surprise Linda with a diamond wedding band, claiming it would be too extravagant.

Linda's sister, Carol, was her matron of honor, and Maryanne and Jacquie her bridesmaids. Billy Drake was Freddy's best man. David Desmond, Maryanne's husband of two years, was an usher, along with Taylor Johnson, a childhood friend of Freddy's from Virginia, where their fathers had done business when Fred was building affordable housing for naval personnel and their families after World War II. He'd worked closely with Taylor's father, a phenomenally wealthy insurance magnate.

Freddy's thirteen-year-old brother, Robert, was his only other sibling to attend. Donald, who was at New York Military Academy, and Elizabeth, who was a college sophomore in Virginia, were told by their father not to make the trip.

The couple planned to honeymoon in Hawaii because, through Linda's association with National, they were able to get a low airfare on a Pan Am flight. After the wedding reception, they spent the night in Miami and left for Los Angeles the next morning. From there they flew to Honolulu. Freddy had planned the whole trip with a travel agent in Brooklyn, and he and Linda had no idea what to expect. Hawaii took their breath away, but there were moments when both of them were frightened by what they had just done.

After the honeymoon, Freddy and Linda moved into a one-bedroom apartment in Sutton Place, an upscale neighborhood on the Upper East Side of Manhattan. Freddy had already been working full time at Trump Management since he graduated from college, and was slated to be his father's deputy at Trump Village, already under construction in Brooklyn. Trump Village was a massive project of seven twenty-three-floor buildings, by far the largest Fred had undertaken. Freddy was on-site five, sometimes six days a week, and Fred wanted the newlyweds to live in one of his Brooklyn buildings. But Freddy wanted some autonomy from the pressures of the business and his family. Even so, he and Linda drove to the House in Jamaica Estates every Wednesday evening to join the rest of his siblings for the compulsory Trump family dinner.

Linda continued to work as a stewardess at National until the day before her wedding, and then, because airlines didn't allow married women to work, she resigned. After the wedding, she found a job as a receptionist at an office in the Chrysler Building, about a twenty-minute walk from their Sutton Place apartment.

Freddy and Linda decided to wait a couple of years before having children. They wanted to travel. While Freddy's mother had taken his sisters, Elizabeth and Maryanne, to Scotland many times over the years to visit her place of birth, she had never brought Freddy. Linda thought it would be good for him to meet his mother's family in Scotland and father's family in Germany.

Only a few months after the honeymoon, however, she discovered she was pregnant. Policy at her workplace prohibited pregnant women from working as receptionists, and as soon as she started to show, Linda quit. She was now a full-time housewife.

It was disappointing having to put off their travel plans, but Linda took the pregnancy in stride. She had grown up believing this was the way it was supposed to be: work, get married, have kids right away, buy a house—and in the early 1960s that was the way things were for most women, by choice, expectation, or lack of opportunity. But the idea of being a dad so soon unnerved Freddy, who was still only twenty-three.

They made the most of their last summer before their first child, a son, was born. Their socializing came to include black-tie fundraisers to benefit Jamaica Hospital, his mother's favorite charity and a place she spent an inordinate amount of time as a patient, originally because of serious complications after her last pregnancy and then because of fractures caused by severe osteoporosis. Mostly, though, Freddy, Linda, and their friends spent glittering evenings at Manhattan clubs and dined at trendy restaurants like La Vie en Rose on Little Neck Parkway.

Freddy's greatest joy was flying his friends out east, where they attended the Clam Fest at Montauk Point, and he taught them how to fish, pilot boats, and shuck clams. Freddy had yet another new boat, which he'd christened *Huggi Bear*, a term of endearment he used for Linda. He kept it in Hewlett Harbor, on the South Shore of Long Island, and he and Linda would sail east to Great South Bay, and sometimes along the inland waterways as far as Peconic Bay, where they visited Billy Drake. These trips became Freddy's escape from the pressures of a newborn son in Jamaica and his father in Brooklyn.

In the Trump Management office on Avenue Z and during their time working together in the field, Freddy had trouble

understanding what his father expected of him—not because
he didn't have the capacity for understanding, but because the
expectations were either ambiguous, self-contradictory, or ri-
diculous. Why did he have to be a killer? Why did he have to
treat their tenants like dirt? Why, in a company that ran like a
well-oiled machine, did this enormously wealthy man feel it
necessary to recycle nails he picked up at his building sites? But
Fred Trump couldn't stand waste. Fred Trump couldn't stand
feeling like he was being taken advantage of. And, it turned out,
Fred Trump couldn't stand delegating responsibility—especially
to somebody he considered his inferior, which, increasingly, is
how he thought of his oldest son.

To get out from under his father's stifling control and blanket disapproval, Freddy applied to TWA, one of the largest airlines in the world and, under the ownership of Howard Hughes, the most glamorous. He was accepted into the first pilot class of 1964. In January, he moved halfway across the country to TWA's five-thousand-acre pilot-training facility a few miles north of Kansas City, Missouri, for four months to train on the Boeing 707, which, already embraced by TWA's greatest rival, Pan Am, was transforming air travel. Linda and sixteen-month-old Fritz joined him two months later.

Of the twelve men in his class, Freddy was one of only two pilots who hadn't received their training in the military. Being peers with navy, air force, and army pilots made it all the more of an accomplishment for him, since he'd spent time around—and looked up to—the officers in the ROTC program at Lehigh. His private training, however, put him at a disadvantage because he had to become familiar with instruments he'd never worked with and learn maneuvers he'd never attempted.

Freddy and Linda spent evenings sitting on the couch in their small living room, Fritz nearby in his crib, while she quizzed him using flash cards on which she'd written the technical terms he needed to commit to memory. There were as many as a dozen different checklists that a crew on the flight deck of a jet had to get through, and the preflight checklist alone included more than thirty items that captain and copilot read aloud in a call-and-response format.

Reading the questions was easy, but it was something else altogether to know how the flaps and slats needed to be deployed.

Freddy could land a puddle jumper—or even a turboprop—in the middle of an airfield in Pennsylvania with his eyes closed. Now he'd be flying jets carrying more than 140 passengers out of and into some of the busiest airports in the country.

Freddy had spent hundreds of hours behind the controls of Douglas DC-7s and Lockheed Constellations, known as Connies, but those were straight-wing turboprops. The new 707s had jet engines instead of propellers and a swept-wing design that improved performance and allowed for higher speeds but also created unfamiliar hazards.

The most dangerous of these was the Dutch roll, which happens when a plane experiences yaw-roll coupling (tail-wagging and side-to-side motion) that can lead inexperienced pilots to panic and overcompensate, potentially resulting in a crash. Very few people on the ground could understand the level of expertise and cool-headedness it required to handle these hazards, and before flight simulators were invented, practical training consisted of flying the actual airplane.

There was nothing frivolous about any of what he learned, and the job fulfilled him in a way that collecting rent and overseeing building projects never could. Like his ROTC and National Guard training, piloting had a clarity that was lacking in his father's real estate business, in which rules could be broken regardless of the well-being of the people involved.

Freddy did so well in the program that when he graduated, TWA assigned him to fly the Logan Airport–LAX route. He, Linda, and Fritz moved to Marblehead, a small harbor town not far from Boston. But four months later, he resigned. Although Freddy could fly a 160-ton aircraft and keep all 180 passengers safe, he could not withstand the pressure his father was putting on him to return to Trump Management. "You're a goddamned chauffeur in the sky," Fred told him when they spoke on the phone. "Dad's embarrassed by you," his much younger brother, Donald, informed him during his only visit to Marblehead. "He tells everybody you're just a glorified bus driver."

The mockery from his family, the amount of time he found himself at loose ends between flights, and the responsibility of being a twenty-six-year-old parent of a two-year-old son took their toll. Freddy started to drink more at the frequent neighborhood parties; he drank when he took the boat out; he drank at home. The stress took an enormous toll on the marriage. Because of the deep shame he felt—at struggling to hold on to his dream, at failing to live up to his father's expectations—he couldn't confide in his wife, leaving him to deal with all of it alone.

When Freddy told Linda he was resigning from TWA, she hadn't seen it coming.

He moved Linda and Fritz back into the Highlander and flew for a couple of regional commuter airlines, one in Albany and one in Oklahoma, but it didn't last. By the end of 1964 he was back at Trump Management working for Fred again. This time it was clear he had no future there. His father had never respected him; after the betrayal of leaving Trump Management, Fred would never trust his namesake again.

I was born in the spring of 1965 to parents who were struggling to regain their equilibrium both as a couple and as individuals with their own problems—Linda with her loneliness and lack of support, Freddy with his fall from grace and his drinking.

Being back at Trump Management full time demoralized Freddy. Between that, the stress of seeing his angry and disdainful father every day, and having two children under the age of three at home, he needed a reprieve. The summer after I turned one, my parents rented a cottage in Montauk. They planned to have Mom, Fritz, and me stay out there from Memorial Day until Labor Day, while Dad, stuck in Brooklyn Monday through Friday, would fly his Piper Cherokee out to the landing strip across from the cottage to join us on the weekends.

The weekdays were long and lonely for both of them, but Freddy, especially, lived for the weekends, which often included invitations for friends to join him on the flight out. Billy and Annamaria, now married, were their most frequent guests.

During the long summer days of 1966, they would take the boat out for a day of deep-sea fishing and grill their catch in the backyard in the evening, or have clambakes on the beach with steamers and cherrystones they bought at a seafood market and shucked themselves. After dark, Freddy set up a portable movie screen and projector, and Freddy and Billy watched W. C. Fields movies while their wives chatted quietly in the dark.

Sometimes it seemed just like old times; except, of course, it wasn't. As the summer wore on, Linda noticed that Freddy was drinking earlier in the day, especially when they took the boat out for long trips.

In June, Linda's parents, Mike and Mary, set out on a long road trip in a van my grandfather had fitted out to accommodate my grandmother's wheelchair. After stopping to see us in Montauk, they planned to visit the rest of the family in Mich-

igan, Minnesota, and Colorado. Nobody said it out loud, but
Mary Clapp didn't think she had long to live and imagined this
might be her last opportunity to see her far-flung family.

They stayed in Montauk for two weeks. My grandmother
was in a great deal of pain and Freddy did everything he could
to cheer her up. Just before my grandparents left, he told his
mother-in-law that when she came back to visit the next year,
he'd have her out on the tennis court.

Mike and Mary Clapp adored their son-in-law. Mike shared
his love of flying, and he'd been in awe of Freddy as soon as he
and Linda arrived in Fort Lauderdale in Freddy's Piper Cherokee. That awe approached something akin to hero worship when
Freddy started flying 707s for TWA.

Mary appreciated how sweet and solicitous Freddy could be,
and he treated her with great gentleness.

His in-laws' love made Freddy feel valued in a way his own
parents, especially his father, never did. But he never felt that he
could unburden himself to them or rely on them for emotional
support. Their admiration blinded them to Freddy's struggles
and the alarming disintegration of their daughter's marriage.

Toward the end of that first summer, Freddy often flew back
from Montauk to New York on Sunday evenings after a long
day of drinking, without waiting to sober up before getting behind the controls. He flew intoxicated even when he had guests
with him. Whenever Linda expressed concern, he waved her off,
insulted that she doubted his skill, which only intensified the
tension between them.

One Sunday he'd been drinking so much that Linda felt she
needed to stop him. "Freddy, you cannot fly like this. You're
going to get yourself or somebody else killed."

He reminded her he was an excellent pilot.

"It doesn't matter how good you are," she said. "You're drunk."

Freddy got close to her and through clenched teeth hissed, "It's none of your goddamn business."

He started throwing his gear into his flight bag while she pleaded with him to wait until the morning to fly back to New York. When he continued to ignore her, she threw her drink in his face. Stunned and angry, he left without saying another word and flew home anyway.

Freddy *was* an excellent pilot, but it wasn't the first time he'd flown when he shouldn't have. He sometimes skipped the preflight inspection. Only a couple of years earlier, he and Linda had had plans to spend the weekend in Bimini. Freddy had leased a plane at Teterboro Airport, a commuter airport in New Jersey, to fly to Norfolk, Virginia, where Taylor Johnson and his wife, Jimbo, would join them, and then the four of them would continue on to the island. The morning of the trip, however, the weather wasn't good.

As they sat in the apartment waiting to get the all clear from the control tower, which took several hours, Freddy drank steadily to pass the time. Despite Linda's misgivings, Freddy drove them the forty-five minutes to the airport. When they arrived, they were well behind schedule, so in order to make up some time, Freddy skipped the preflight check. He was usually meticulous, and his lapse in judgment was, at least as far as Linda knew, unheard of—the pilot or flight engineer always checks the plane, and on a plane that small, the preflight inspection falls to the pilot, especially if the plane doesn't belong to him.

The takeoff and flight went smoothly, but when they approached the Norfolk airport, an air traffic controller waved them off. The plane had a flat tire, and they were told to circle the airport a few times while an emergency truck sprayed foam on the runway in case the plane's engines caught fire during the crash landing (there is no other way to land a plane without landing gear). It's possible that the wheel had been damaged during the flight, but it was also possible that Freddy might have detected the problem if he'd done the preflight check, a fact that didn't escape either of them.

As they made their approach, Linda's stewardess training kicked in: she took the pens out of Freddy's shirt pocket and stowed them so they didn't impale anybody. Freddy landed the plane without incident, and as they waited for the emergency crew to give the all clear, Freddy saluted her. "Good job," Linda said, and then they shook hands. But before meeting the Johnsons, they agreed to fly commercial the rest of the way to Bimini.

Linda was alarmed at the increasing frequency of these types of incidents, and by the end of the summer of '66, she was exhausted from entertaining, taking care of two small children almost single-handedly, and worrying about her husband's drinking and erratic behavior.

It was a relief to be back in Jamaica that autumn. Freddy, however, already had his sights set on going to Montauk again the following year.

Dad traded the Piper Cherokee for a Cessna and bought a Chrisovich, a thirty-foot boat with a tuna tower, which he could drive much farther offshore for the kind of deep-sea fishing—for tuna and swordfish—he preferred. He often skirted the United States' sovereign maritime zone, twelve miles out, where he and Linda and whatever friends were with them saw sea turtles and whales. Once a humpback breached so close to them that Freddy, usually unflappable, gunned the engine because, as he later told Linda, he was terrified the whale might capsize the boat.

During another trip with Billy and Annamaria, they spotted a Soviet naval vessel. Stone-faced sailors lined the railing, probably not knowing what to make of the skinny blond guy driving the boat, the other one sitting in the fishing seat with a beer, and the two beautiful bikini-clad women standing on the tuna tower smiling and waving at them.

Only a few years after the Cuban Missile Crisis, the Cold War between the United States and the Soviet Union was intensifying, and the smart thing to do would have been to reverse direction quietly. But egged on by Billy, Freddy buzzed the vessel while Annamaria shouted, "Do svidaniya!" at the sailors, who, luckily for the four Americans, ignored them.

Linda was still lonely during the week, but now that Fritz and I were a little older, there was more she could do with us. My parents had also become friendly with their next-door neighbors, Ricky and Gail Schneider. Like most of the husbands, Ricky, a neurosurgeon, only came out on the weekends, so Gail, whose kids were teenagers, also had a lot of time on her hands.

She confided to Linda that Ricky had a drinking problem. Linda, relieved to have somebody to confide in, unburdened herself to Gail, who knew that Freddy was struggling and the marriage was in trouble. Gail was older, so even though she and Ricky continued to face similar difficulties, she had more experience and was better able to take things in stride. To the extent it was possible, she helped Linda negotiate the land mines put in her path by marriage to an alcoholic who seemed to have no support.

Dad still lived for the weekends, but as the summer wore on it became harder for him to unwind after he landed the plane at the Montauk airport. When it seemed things couldn't get any worse, Fred and Mary Trump decided to visit. Freddy suspected his father was only coming to check up on him.

Freddy spent the entire time worrying that Fred was going to find out that he'd bought another, more expensive plane and another, much more expensive boat. Linda worried her in-laws would discover how bad Freddy's drinking had gotten. In typical Trump style, however, my grandparents left as soon as the lunch my mother prepared for them was over. They had no interest in seeing the town or going near the water. Freddy and Linda's secrets were safe, at least for the time being, and the release of tension as soon as the limo pulled out of the dirt driveway onto the main street was palpable. Freddy slumped into a chair on the porch and, in a concession to how stressful the visit had been, Linda went into the kitchen and fixed them both a drink.

That moment of camaraderie wouldn't last. When they returned to Jamaica after Labor Day, my mother promised herself she would not be going back to Montauk. Dad, on the other hand, was determined to get back to Montauk the next year. But there wasn't going to be a next year.

———————

My father's parents had never approved of Linda. Because of her working-class upbringing and, perhaps, their low opinion of Freddy, they assumed from the start that she was a gold digger who glommed on to the first rich man she met. Given my grandmother's own upbringing as the tenth child of a crofter on a tiny island forty miles off the west coast of Scotland who worked as a domestic servant when she first arrived in New York, the double standard was a bit much.

But it didn't matter. In the end, they would fail each other in very specific ways: he couldn't take care of her, and she couldn't set him free. They both ended up trapped in ways that neither of them could have imagined.

A few months later, I woke up in the middle of the night to the sound of my father's laughter. I slid out of bed, the moon so bright outside my window that I had no trouble finding my way to the door. I stood on my tiptoes to reach the doorknob, and just as I slid through the doorway and stepped up to the threshold of my parents' bedroom, my mother started screaming.

My father, who had backed himself against the double chest of drawers, was pointing a rifle at my mother and threatening to blow her head off. She sat on the bed, leaning as far away from him as she could, her hand held up in front of her face.

He was out of his mind with drunkenness, and the laughter injected a note of perversity that I think terrorized my mother as much as the presence of the gun.

Neither of my parents saw me, and before they could, I ran back to my room and hopped in bed as if nothing had happened at all. The experience jolted me into time and memory; it still hums with a mild current, alive, unprocessed and intact.

Before this, there had been only impressions—my cheek pressed against my mother's tanned shoulder, warm from the sun, and the intoxicating smell of chlorine and Coppertone as she swam through the cool water with me on her back, arms clasped around her; the rough stubble of my father's cheek and the dark smell of tobacco, the sharp scent of alcohol that clung to him. These isolated islands of sensation—inchoate, beyond language—carried no weight, free from the burden of meaning. But, not yet three, I was sensitive to the ways in which the people around me orbited each other, clashed with each other, and sometimes disappeared, leaving only the echoes of their instabilities.

10

After my parents moved back to Jamaica from Marblehead, they had become friendly with four other couples in the neighborhood, all of whom lived within a three-block radius in buildings owned by my grandfather. The relationships revolved mostly around their all having kids about the same age, and after my parents split, my mother inherited them. The women had been the ones who spent the most time together—taking the kids in their strollers to the park for walks, planning our birthdays, and going to each other's parties.

Now a single mother, Linda also grew closer with some of the neighbors who shared our corner of the ninth floor, especially Meghan Spencer, a tall, thin woman who looked like she'd never spent time in the sun. She always wore sleeveless sheath dresses and kept her light brown hair swept off her forehead with a black or tortoiseshell headband. I barely remember her husband, Jim, except that he was a solid, quiet man who wore glasses with heavy black frames.

They were a mild, boring couple, but I think it was Meghan's equanimity that drew my mother to her after her own marriage became more volatile. (Jim and Meghan eventually moved to a house far out on Long Island. They divorced years later, and I wasn't surprised to learn that they continued to live together in the same house but slept on different floors. It seemed like the kind of passionless thing they would do.)

Meghan started teaching me how to read when I was three, and we spent a lot of time together with *The Cat in the Hat* and *Green Eggs and Ham*. During our lessons, we sat side by side on the couch in her living room or ours, she with a cup of tea

WHO COULD EVER LOVE YOU   37

perched with its saucer on her knee and me with the book in my
lap, tracing the words with my finger. She taught me how to create
islands of calm, but more than that, she opened up worlds I could
not only escape to but would eventually inhabit. I was drawn to
her quiet, no-nonsense approach. In those hours she spent pa-
tiently sitting on the couch with me as I sounded out syllables and
she hummed her approval or gently corrected me, I felt a great deal
of affection for her. And because of her persistence, I was able to
read by myself by the time I was three and a half.

Mrs. Kohner could not have been more different from
Meghan. An older widow with a dyed black bouffant, oversize
Coco Chanel eyeglasses that she kept attached to a long chain
around her neck, and a sarcastic edge, she lived in a one-bedroom
at the end of the hallway.

Her husband, the inventor of the board game Trouble, had
been dead for years. If she had children, I never saw them. She
seemed lonely, and I had the sense that her fortunes had changed
for the worse after her husband died. She was not shy about her
resentment at having been reduced to living in a rental building
in Jamaica, Queens.

Mrs. Kohner also happened to be a chain-smoking alcoholic.
When sober, she could be gloomy and misanthropic. But she
took my mother under her less-than-maternal wing, and the
two of them spent long afternoons alternately commiserating
with each other and railing against their lots in life.

My mother's parties were pretty mild affairs, but Mrs. Kohner
was almost always the life of them. I'd seen enough of my father's
drinking to know what drunkenness was, and Mrs. Kohner never
failed to get absolutely plastered. My mother tried to cut her off
and encourage her to go home, but Mrs. Kohner—who, when
sober, didn't have any particular interest in me—always insisted
she be allowed to put me to bed.

She followed me and my mother into my room, and after I jumped into bed and my mother tucked me in, Mrs. Kohner sat unsteadily on the edge of my bed, a lit cigarette in one hand, a highball in the other. Mom went back to her other guests. As Mrs. Kohner talked and smoked and drank, she leaned heavily on my twin bed, pinning me beneath the comforter, so I couldn't shift my little body away from her, her cigarette ash, or the occasional splash of scotch.

In addition to her eyeglasses, Mrs. Kohner wore long necklaces fashioned out of large, highly polished river stones, and as she swayed back and forth—putting her drink on the floor or getting closer to me when she had a particularly interesting point to make (I don't remember a word the woman said)—the stones clicked together, marking her unsteadiness. She had a guttural, phlegmy smoker's cough, and the way she was talking and slurring and falling and catching herself from falling, I lived in terror that she was going to throw up all over me. From time to time, my mother came in to check on us. I tried to signal to her with my eyes that I wanted this to stop, but she only shrugged and looked at me helplessly before going back to the party. What, after all, could she possibly do?

This was my first lesson in propriety. Mrs. Kohner would stay as long as she wanted. If she got cigarette ashes or scotch on me, so be it. If she threw up on me or set my bed on fire, at least we hadn't made her feel unwelcome.

11

My parents didn't have a formal separation agreement until 1970, so for the first couple of years after they split up, Dad came to the Highlander on the weekends when he was able to. This schedule worked for him. I think being on his own was a relief. Being a part-time father suited him: he could have fun with us without the burden of too much responsibility and for a strictly limited amount of time.

Sometimes we stayed in the apartment, but only if my mother wasn't home—she had a hard time being in the same room with him. On warm days we walked down to South Jamaica, Dad carrying me on his shoulders and my brother trying to keep up with Dad's long, easy stride. If there was a good movie playing, we went to the Loews theater on Jamaica Avenue, an ornate 1920s movie palace festooned with decorative pilasters and finials and cherubs.

By the late sixties it had seen better days, but it still retained some of its classical grandeur. I was in awe of the gilt-edged seats, sweeping balcony, and massive red velvet curtains; it might have been sacrilegious to watch a movie like Jerry Lewis's *Hook, Line & Sinker* in such a place. But I loved being there, especially on hot, cloudy days, when the three of us could sit in the cool dark air together and alone at the same time. And maybe Dad, for a couple of hours at least, could lose himself.

He also usually swung by to pick us up one night a week. Sometimes we went to the House, but it was better—easier, less fraught—when he took us to Dante's, a little Italian place not too far from the Highlander on one of the quieter sections of Union Turnpike.

There was a sameness about those dinners that comforted me—we ordered spaghetti and meatballs, and Fritz and I fought over the jukebox. Not over the songs we played, which were always the same—"Raindrops Keep Fallin' on My Head," "Cracklin' Rosie," and "Sweet Caroline"—but over who got to put the coins in the slot and who got to push the buttons. Since we were going to keep picking the same songs to play again and again, it didn't matter. "Take turns," Dad said, sliding us some more change across the heavily varnished wood table.

If my mother and father hadn't yet figured out a way to be in the same room without getting into a fight, my father and grandfather *had* figured out that there would be no salvaging their relationship at all. My grandfather had won, and Dad couldn't move on. But there was still tension between them, which I could feel, even if I didn't understand it, whenever we went to the House.

After a dinner that we'd eaten in the breakfast room, we moved to the dimly lit library, a room with no books, in which the family spent the most time. Dad sat with my grandmother on the love seat by the bay window, and I stood next to my grandfather's knee while he taught me and my brother how to spell words like "arithmetic" and "Mississippi" backward and forward, or add long columns of four- or five-digit numbers that he wrote on a white pad of cheap scratch paper with one of his blue Flair markers. By the time he finished writing the numbers down, he had already solved the problem in his head. Like magic.

12

On a beautiful, desultory day in early autumn, I was hanging out with my friends in the parking lot of the Belcrest, another building owned by Fred Trump, which stood diagonally across 164th Street from the Highlander. The older kids were in school, so it was a small group of us, with nothing to do until lunchtime.

Andre, a boy in my building who had just started first grade at Kew-Forest, a private school in Forest Hills where my brother, Fritz, and cousin David, Maryanne's son, were already students, had given me a few primary readers that he'd outgrown. I'd been reading for almost a year, but these books, pristine except for his name written on the flyleaf, were mine, and I was very proud of them. I brought them with me to show them off. But, as riveting as Spot may have been, my friends soon lost interest and I put the books down on the curb. We started searching for a good stone and a stick of chalk so we could play hopscotch.

Christina, a small blond girl, hair always in pigtails, whom I knew from the Belcrest pool, picked up one of the books and started reading it. I didn't think anything of it until she said, "These are my books." She sounded so certain I thought she was making an honest mistake. I told her she was wrong and continued my search for a stone. But then she announced to everybody that I was a liar. I walked over to her and tried to take the book back from her, but she pulled it tightly to her body.

"OK," I said, picking up another book. "See?" I pointed to Andre's name. "My friend Andre gave these to me. They're not yours."

She lowered her arms, I thought to give the book back, but

she dropped it on the ground and, without any warning, started hitting me. I was already a tomboy: nobody intimidated me and almost nothing scared me, so I hit her back. We were both four, and very small, so I'm not sure how much damage we could have done to each other, but, in context, it was a knock-down, drag-out fight with a lot of slapping, hair pulling, and cheering from our spectators.

Christina's apartment in the Belcrest had a view of the parking lot, and her mother must have been looking out the window to keep an eye on us when the fight started, because all of a sudden, a woman was running toward us. For a split second I was relieved that an adult was coming to stop the fight and give me my books back. She pulled us apart, neither of us too much the worse for wear. I was about to explain what had happened when Christina's mom grabbed me by the hair and slapped me hard across my face.

The shock of it made me forget the books whose honor I'd been fighting to defend. As soon as she let go of me, I ran home, half-blinded by tears, across 165th Street, across Highland Avenue, down the brick steps and across the flagstone entryway that cut through the oak trees casting their perpetual shade across the front entrance of the Highlander, through the lobby, past the doorman, and into the elevator. By the time my mother opened the front door, I was sobbing. I collapsed into her arms and tried to catch my breath. She was so alarmed she looked me over to see if I'd been hurt. She hushed me and begged me to tell her what had happened. After I did, she took my hand and walked toward the kitchen, where she promised me milk and cookies.

But before we could get there, the intercom buzzed. The doorman announced there was a woman in the lobby who wanted to come upstairs. I knew who it was before he clarified, "She says she's from the Belcrest."

I don't know if I expected anything in that moment, but what I didn't expect was for my mother to say, "Send her up."

When my mother opened the front door, the woman stood there looking embarrassed. She held my books out to me, but I had planted myself behind my mother and wouldn't let go of her. I was terrified.

After I ran away from the Belcrest parking lot, Christina's mother figured out what had really happened. She had made a huge mistake, she said. She was sorry Christina had lied. She hoped I could forgive both of them. My cheek still stung, but I didn't feel scared anymore. I was angry.

I waited for my mother to light into her, to tell her to stay away from me, to challenge her to a duel. Instead, she pulled me in front of her and said, "We accept your apology." The woman, who until now had been standing in the hallway, smiled. She stepped over the threshold, looked down at me, and held out her hand.

"Go ahead, Mary." A gentle push put me a step closer to my enemy. "Shake hands." When I didn't move, she said, more sternly this time, as if I had done something wrong, "Shake hands."

So, I did.

That was my second lesson in propriety. And my first lesson in betrayal.

13

My mother needed something to do. Fritz was in school full time and I had started preschool—only a few hours in the morning, but it still left her with too much time on her hands. She didn't like being at loose ends.

My grandparents were on the board of Booth Memorial Hospital, which was run by the Salvation Army, and my grandmother donated money to the hospital's Women's Auxiliary. The hospital was only a fifteen-minute drive from Jamaica, so, already familiar with the organization through fundraisers and luncheons she'd attended, Mom joined the Women's Auxiliary and began volunteering several hours a week in the afternoons.

Mrs. Lombardi, a widow in the neighborhood, had started to babysit some of the neighborhood kids as a way to supplement her income. Her husband had died recently, leaving her with debt and five children, two of whom were still under eighteen. The Lombardis lived a couple of blocks away from us on a dead-end street in a converted two-family house right next to an overgrown section of the park. A few days a week, after picking me up from preschool, my mother dropped me off there. Sometimes there were a couple of other kids around my age, but usually it was just me and Mrs. Lombardi until her teenagers Antonio and Teresa got home from high school. I rarely saw the two oldest daughters, even though Angela, an already divorced bookkeeper, lived in the attic, and Maria, a junior at Queens College, lived in the basement. Luca was a firefighter who had graduated from high school a year earlier. He still lived at home when he wasn't at the fire station and, despite his job, was still a big kid struggling to grow a mustache.

The Lombardi house always smelled of oregano and garlic. When it was just Mrs. Lombardi and me, I stayed with her in the gloomy kitchen, which had been painted a greyish green, where on rainy days it felt like we were underwater. She lifted me onto the center island and I perched there and chatted with her while she cooked.

The best days were when she made meatballs. Once she added the ground beef, bread crumbs, grated parmesan, eggs, parsley, garlic, and pepper to a dented stainless-steel prep bowl, she rose onto her toes and drove both hands into the bowl as if propulsion were an essential ingredient to get the mixing started. I watched mesmerized as the meat slid through her fingers and the eggs melded with everything else until they seemed to disappear. What most amazed me was watching her roll the resulting mixture into perfect spheres with the practiced hands of an artisan.

When she turned to the stove and placed the olive oil to heat in an enormous and battered old skillet, I skimmed the remnants of raw ingredients from the side of the bowl with my finger and licked it clean.

When the oil in the pan began to ripple, Mrs. Lombardi helped me jump down from the island. I stood next to her as she placed each meatball delicately in the skillet and watched as the oil sizzled and jumped. When they were done cooking, she placed them on paper towels she'd laid on the counter, and as soon as they'd cooled down, she let me have one.

I preferred to be alone with her, there in the kitchen where she taught me about the different kinds of pastas or showed me, step by step, how to make Italian bread from scratch. Mrs. Lombardi seemed sad sometimes, but I was comfortable with sadness and knew when to let the quiet settle between us.

Sometimes she watched other kids in the neighborhood.

Annie Bea and Barb were there more than anyone else. If it rained, we stayed in the small front room just off the foyer where Mrs. Lombardi kept stacks of board games, like Don't Break the Ice, Candyland, and the extra game of Trouble that Mrs. Kohner had given us for the second Christmas in a row. Otherwise, we were outside playing freeze tag or Mother, may I in the driveway.

On days when I was the only one left by the time school let out, Antonio, Teresa, and Luca, if he was home, let me tag along with them to Goose Pond Park, our nickname for Captain Tilly Park. If I had my fishing rod with me (the one my father had bought for me at the Woolworth's a couple of blocks from the movie theater), they grabbed a couple of slices of Wonder Bread that I could use for bait.

I wasn't allowed in the park after sunset, even with them, so if my mother worked late at Booth Memorial, I stayed with the big kids, dressed in their army jackets with POW/MIA patches and tie-dye shirts, in the Lombardis' backyard. While they smoked and set off cherry bombs and bottle rockets in the early evenings, the Beatles, Steppenwolf, and Sly and the Family Stone played on the transistor radio Luca let us use when he had a shift at the firehouse.

I was there so often in the afternoons after preschool let out that their house began to feel like a second home, and Mrs. Lombardi and the kids, especially Teresa and Antonio and Luca, like family.

Antonio, the handsome one, the one who was popular and outgoing, the one I loved not as much as Luca and Teresa but almost as much, started bringing me to the small sunny room just off the front hallway. This was where my friends and I played board games. This was where I tried to pound out songs like "Volga Boatman" on the old upright piano.

I don't remember how many times Antonio took me to that room, but I know why he stopped. One afternoon, as the lace curtains blew gently in the late spring breeze, we stood there half-naked. When Antonio reached out to me, because I was too scared to touch him, his mother opened the door.

It seemed as though nothing moved, and nobody breathed. Then she leapt across the room and pulled us apart. "You!" she screamed. To him or to me, I didn't know. She planted her palm against her teenaged son's chest and he stumbled backward over his lowered jeans. Then she grabbed my arm and pulled me toward the door.

As usual, I got the signals crossed, because when we reached the threshold, Mrs. Lombardi smacked me across my bare ass, pushed me into the foyer, and slammed the door.

I pulled up my pants but had no idea what to do or where to go. Mrs. Lombardi and Antonio stayed in the room for a long time. I let myself out the front door and sat on the steps until, as the darkness gathered, my mother came to get me.

Mrs. Lombardi never said anything to my parents or anyone else, as far as I know, about what had happened. I assumed I'd done something wrong, so I was relieved I didn't get in trouble.

I continued to go to that house practically every weekday for the next three or four years. But I was never alone with Antonio again.

14

The road ended where the water should have been.

We'd been driving for almost eight hours when my mother turned right off of Route 6A, the main street that divided the Cape Cod town of Brewster in half, onto Linnell Landing, a narrow road that sloped down through the pine trees toward the bay.

It was 1970, and we were there to drop my brother off at Monomoy, an all-boys sleepaway camp, for the first time. On the left, private homes—neat cottages and bungalows, most shingled with weathered cedar—were set back from the road, and on the right, the camp's low-profile utilitarian buildings, painted army-issue grey, sat in the shadow of the pines. Fritz would be spending the next two months there.

My mother continued down the hill to the small municipal parking lot next to Linger Longer, a group of cottages the camp owned where she and I would be staying for a few days after dropping Fritz off. When we emerged from the cover of pines into the clear sunshine of midday, we expected to see the bay, where, we'd been told, campers swam and sailed every day. To find this empty basin of flattened damp sand was a bit of a blow.

As soon as my mother parked the car, I jumped out and ran to the beach. My mother and brother, his hand raised to shield his eyes from the sun, followed.

The day was still and hot, and the heat shimmered and bounced off the rocks in waves.

The beach was empty of people but for an older couple, fully dressed except for their bare feet. As they walked past us, the man said, "Don't worry—it'll come back. Always does." A few sailboats, listing against the blue of the sky, nestled in the sand, their sails furled tightly against their booms, seemed to confirm this.

The woman looked at us from beneath her wide-brimmed straw hat trimmed with a colorful striped grosgrain ribbon and hitched her thumb at the flats. "Low tide—the best babysitter on the planet," she said to my mother.

I started to run toward the nearest jetty, but my mother called me back. We had to bring the bags in and take Fritz to his cabin. By the time we returned, maybe the water would have, too.

After we dropped Fritz off, my mother and I were invited to take a tour of Wono, the girls' camp half a mile down the road. Unlike Monomoy, which stretched out under the shadows of tall evergreens over blankets of pine needles that filled the sea air with their sharp scent, Wono was brighter, much of it open to the sky. The two entrances were separated by one hundred yards along 6A, and the campus itself unfolded over fifty acres of sloping green lawns, clusters of cabins, dirt pathways, and paths strewn with wood chips all the way to the bay.

My mother parked in front of a large white house, and we went into the office to meet our guide, a junior counselor dressed in white shorts and a white T-shirt with the Wono logo emblazoned on the upper left chest. She pointed out the archery range, and on our way to the beach, we passed a massive dining hall, an outdoor theater, groups of three and four cabins clustered together, and tennis courts. By the time we reached the boathouse, where the sails and boat tackle were stored, I was asking my mother if I could return as a camper the following summer.

"Camp rules say you have to be seven," she said. I found that unacceptable but didn't say anything and walked ahead of them to hide my disappointment.

Beyond the boathouse, a wide path between the dunes on

either side opened onto the beach. As promised, the water was returning. The flats had become sandbars, white as bone, and the bright blues and greens of the bay darkened as the tide came in.

I climbed one of the dunes, steep and high, and stood amid the waist-high seagrass. The lighthouse at the tip of Provincetown, less than thirty nautical miles across the bay, glimmered in the sun. The fleet of sailboats, lifted by the incoming tide, strained against their mooring lines, bows pointed into the wind. As the water rose, the wind picked up and the halyards and shackles tapped rhythmically against the masts, a sound that comforted me and seemed to extend a promise.

I wasn't yet aware, at least not in any conscious way, that anything crucial had been missing in my life until I saw those boats. I had an almost preternatural confidence in myself and a certainty—I was so certain—about what I wanted. I was capable of great joy and, more than anything, I moved easily through the world. But in the last year alone, in that little room with the piano and lace curtains, I'd also learned too much about betrayal and the harsh reality that nowhere is safe.

But I felt safe *here*. I had no intention of waiting two years to return. I was determined to be back the next summer as a camper.

I stood on the dunes and surveyed my kingdom.

15

Over the course of that summer, after two and a half years of separation, my parents finally got around to finalizing their divorce. The terms of my mother's alimony and child support, as well as their custody agreement, were set.

The finality of it shut down hope of reconciliation. I don't think either of my parents wanted to get back together—however they moved on, they were going to be moving on separately, while still tied together by the shared responsibility of parenthood. But they might still have loved each other. Maybe that was one of the reasons my mother was so angry—she would never be able to trust my father again, and she hated him for it.

Dad, who'd become more passive the longer he lived in my grandparents' house, believed he deserved whatever he got. Even if he wanted to, he couldn't have broached the idea of trying to make things with Linda work. The divorce, and everything it entailed, destabilized both of them, at least for a while. Mom became edgy and short-tempered. Dad had been trying to get well enough to move into his own place for the first time since he'd left us, but he became despondent and withdrawn.

His life had come to consist of the menial and meaningless grind of working at my grandfather's office on Avenue Z, sporadic attempts to get sober, and long stretches when he couldn't even try. It didn't help that he'd become increasingly isolated from his friends in the years since the summers in Montauk came to an end.

Billy and Annamaria had moved farther east to a house on Long Island, so he rarely saw them anymore, either. But shortly after the papers had been signed in 1970, Annamaria invited Freddy to dinner.

When Annamaria opened the door, she was shocked by what she saw. Freddy had always been thin, but he'd lost a lot of weight. Always a sharp dresser, he now looked bedraggled and desperately in need of comfort.

Annamaria had prepared his favorite meal—rare roast beef and potatoes—but when the three of them sat down to eat, Freddy did little more than push the food around his plate. Mostly, he drank. They didn't speak much during the meal. Annamaria and Billy's marriage was coming to its own bitter end, and the occasion didn't lend itself to small talk. After the meal was over, Billy left to watch television.

Freddy and Annamaria had known each other since her family moved to Jamaica Estates in the early 1960s, much to my grandfather's great chagrin. At that time, Jamaica Estates was almost 100 percent white, and Fred Trump was scandalized that Italians were allowed to move in.

Freddy didn't share his father's prejudices—he'd even joined a fraternity at Lehigh that, until he pledged, had never had a non-Jewish member—and he and Annamaria had quickly become friends. They became closer when she started dating Billy. Along with Linda, Freddy's fraternity brothers, and other friends in the neighborhood, they spent a lot of time on Freddy's boat or at Billy's summer house on the Peconic Bay. In addition to the time the couples spent in Montauk, Annamaria and Billy were also frequent visitors to Marblehead during the brief time my father flew for TWA. They had more fun in the years before Freddy and Linda split up than most people had in a lifetime.

Annamaria thought Freddy was one of the best men she'd ever known. Most people who knew him before everything started falling apart felt the same way. Annamaria understood the Trump family dynamics in a way few people did, which in turn made Freddy feel she understood him. Freddy had nothing in common with his father or Donald, which is one of the reasons they rejected him. They liked to pretend he was a joke, somebody only interested in a good time who couldn't buckle down to do real work. But Annamaria knew Freddy was accomplished in ways his father and brother would never be.

Like Freddy's other friends, Annamaria found my grandfather, whom everybody referred to as the Old Man, cold and intimidating. When she first encountered Donald, he was a cocky, rude teenager who was intensely jealous of his older brother. Donald didn't have any friends, so she felt sorry for him, but whenever they included him, they regretted it. Nobody in Freddy's circle could bear to be around this arrogant, self-important, humorless kid.

Over the years, Annamaria watched Donald evolve into an even more arrogant adult with a widening cruel streak. Everything got worse for Freddy when Donald joined Trump Management after graduating from college in 1968. Fred, who'd frozen Freddy out even before he left the company to join TWA, gave Donald a salary that far surpassed anything he'd ever paid his oldest son, along with perks—a car, a driver, bonuses, credit for work he didn't even do—he'd never considered giving Freddy.

In a year, Fred would make Donald, then only twenty-four years old, president of the company, effectively ending any possibility for my father's advancement. By 1970, none of that mattered; Freddy had given up.

Annamaria knew that one of the reasons, perhaps the main reason, Freddy had fallen so far was not Fred's obvious preference for his much younger, much less worthy son, but his equally obvious disdain for and cruelty toward his namesake. There was literally nothing Freddy could do to change his father's feelings toward him, which only made it worse.

While Freddy described the misery of working for the Old

Man, and how heartbroken he was to be apart from his children, Annamaria realized that all she could do was listen. As the night wore on, Freddy kept drinking and Annamaria insisted he spend the night.

The affection and respect between the two friends were sincere and deep, and it would have done him a world of good if they could have stayed friends. But after she divorced Billy, that would be impossible. Anyway, Freddy couldn't imagine that he would ever have the strength to find his way back. At thirty-two, he was already lost.

16

My brother and I didn't know about the official end of the marriage until Fritz returned from his first summer at camp. One day, out of the blue, my mother sat us down at the dining room table and very solemnly told us that she and Dad were now divorced. This meant that he would never live with us again. She also explained that "visitation" meant we'd be seeing Dad more regularly. "If"—she couldn't help herself—"he figures out how to pull himself together."

As far as I could tell, nothing was going to change about the way we'd been living for the past two and a half years.

Mom bowed her head, and I was afraid she was going to cry. Fritz didn't move, so I hopped down from my chair, wrapped my arms around her shoulders, and stroked her cheek. She squeezed my arm, smiled unconvincingly, and said, "We're going to be OK."

She turned to my brother, who hadn't yet reacted. This surprised me. In some ways he was more outgoing than I was, but he was also older and knew Dad in a way I had never gotten to.

"Fritz, I know this is hard. I've arranged for you—for both of you—to talk to a doctor. You can tell him how you feel just in case you're upset about anything."

He said nothing about it one way or the other, and I wasn't upset. Even so, a few days later, we were in the car on our way to see Dr. Julius Rice, a psychiatrist.

Dr. Rice, she explained, did something called therapy—all we had to do was talk and be honest about our feelings and he could help us "work through them." I didn't know what that meant.

My parents had gone to see Dr. Rice after they'd returned to New York from Marblehead. The move, or rather the way it had come about, had put a lot of stress on their marriage, and Dad's drinking made everything worse. Dr. Rice, Mom said, had been very helpful. In addition to seeing them as a couple, he had also seen them individually. Decades later, my mother told me that during one of his last sessions with her, Dr. Rice broke a cardinal rule of couples counseling when he told her that Freddy was far too immature to be a father or husband. In his professional opinion, she should end the marriage because it was never going to work between her and Freddy.

Dr. Rice worked in a small office building in Queens. We had to be buzzed into the waiting room, where the receptionist told us to take a seat; Dr. Rice was still with a patient. After a few minutes, the phone rang. After the receptionist hung up, she told us the doctor would see us now. Mom went back out to the car to wait.

Nobody had come out of Dr. Rice's office, so I was a little surprised to find him alone. He was an older man—probably in his forties—with a large head and dark hair slicked back off his high forehead. He wore a suit with a sweater underneath his jacket. The air conditioner was on and the room was cold. He explained that patients left by a different door so they didn't have to run into anybody in the waiting room. For privacy reasons. He smiled, showing large teeth.

He took his place behind the desk and pointed to two chairs across from him, indicating that's where we should sit. I still didn't know why we were there, but the separate entrance and exit, the crowded bookcase that covered an entire wall, and Dr. Rice's South African accent all intrigued me.

Dr. Rice explained what he knew of my parents' situation.

My mother, he claimed, was concerned we might be upset about the divorce. He wanted to know if that was the case. Normally, I would have chimed in, but Fritz was quiet, so I stayed quiet, too. As Dr. Rice kept asking questions, I looked at my brother, ready to follow his lead. But other than shrugging his shoulders now and again, he kept insisting everything was fine.

I'm not sure whether Dr. Rice didn't believe him, or if he thought our unwillingness to talk pointed to a deeper problem, but after that first session, he took a different tack with us.

"What do you know," he asked, "about reproduction?"

I was five—that word didn't register. I looked at him blankly.

He pushed his chair back from his desk and went to the bookshelf. He pulled down a heavy, serious-looking textbook that was as thick as the Queens Yellow Pages. After he sat down again, he flipped through the pages until he found what he was looking for.

"Do you," he asked, leaning forward slightly, "know how relationships between men and women work?"

Obviously, in terms of my experience with my parents, relationships between men and women did not work, but I had a feeling that wasn't what he had in mind. Fritz tightened his grip on the edge of his chair.

"Here." Dr. Rice turned the book toward us so we could see the pages. On one side was an illustration of an anatomically correct man and on the other an anatomically correct woman.

"Do you know what this is called?" He took his silver pen and pointed to one of the woman's breasts. Neither one of us answered. My brother blushed so furiously, I could feel the heat coming off of his face.

"No? What about this?"

For the rest of the session, Dr. Rice asked us to identify parts of the human reproductive system. When we stayed silent, he turned to pages with close-up images of all of those things we refused to name and then named them for us, very precisely.

Neither of us wanted to see Dr. Rice again, but when we resisted, Mom told us he thought we were making progress but still needed to work on a few things.

It turns out what Dr. Rice wanted us to "work on" was saying the words out loud.

My parents were both fairly repressed people. I'd never heard any of the words Dr. Rice kept repeating. I'd never seen either of my parents undressed. But I'd seen Antonio. Whenever my turn came to say the unfamiliar, yet vaguely ominous, terms out loud, I steeled myself and said them quickly, without flinching.

If I'd been alone, I might have brazened my way through, because there was no way for me to understand, in isolation, that anything Dr. Rice was doing was wrong. Fritz, on the other hand, struggled. When he eventually did force himself to speak, it was as if doing so caused him physical pain, his mortification was so palpable.

I didn't know what Fritz, who was eight at the time, knew; I didn't know what, if anything, he'd experienced that caused such an intense reaction, but these interactions with Dr. Rice scarred him, and watching his humiliation scarred me, too, though in a different way. I didn't know how to reconcile my confident older brother, whom I adored and looked up to, with this shamed boy.

Therapy, like a family, is a closed system, so nothing that happened in those sessions with Dr. Rice ever escaped that room. The idea that anybody else could ever know was unthinkable.

17

Dad had just "gotten back," our code for his return from rehab. When he said he was stopping by to drop off some checks for Mom, she told him to meet us at the dance studio in South Jamaica where I was taking ballet and tap lessons with the daughters of her Jamaica friends.

When the lesson ended, Dad was waiting for us on the sidewalk, standing in a pool of sunlight. He looked good, as if he'd been scrubbed clean. His cheeks had filled out and had some color in them; his clothes fit better, as if he'd put on some weight. On the walk home, he extolled the virtues of orange juice and told us he finally found an apartment so Fritz and I could spend weekends with him.

In those years, Dad was in rehab or the hospital fairly often—I didn't always know which. After a serious case of lobar pneumonia landed him in the ICU in 1963, he was prone to that illness, and smoking two packs of cigarettes a day didn't help. Since he'd returned to New York and Trump Management, his drinking controlled him at least as often as he controlled it.

As far as I knew, Dad had been living in the House since Mom had the locks to the apartment changed, something my grandfather had done at her request—without complaint, for once. Dad had cleared out one side of the attic, set up an army cot, and put a six-inch black-and-white TV on top of his old National Guard trunk, which doubled as a coffee table.

I don't know why he opted to live in the attic, although, with its southern exposure, it was bigger and more brightly lit than his childhood bedroom—a small, dark, depressing room we called "the Cell." Being in the attic also made it easier to avoid my grandfather when he was in the House.

Over the course of the next few years, Dad would move back into the House whenever he came out of rehab. If he was well enough, or if my grandfather wasn't home, he'd join us in the library on Sunday mornings to watch reruns of Abbott and Costello movies on WPIX (Channel 11 in New York City). While we waited for the movie to start, we guessed which one they'd be showing; I always held out hope for *Hold That Ghost* or *The Time of Their Lives*.

The television in the library was nestled in the built-in bookcase on the far side of the room, which held little else other than photographs. A solitary chair a few feet away was reserved for my grandmother. By the time "Popcorn," by Hot Butter, started playing, we had already fought over who would get Gam's seat, the only one in the room with a good view of the television. Whoever won also got control of the broomstick that Dad had fashioned into a remote control. Gam's severe osteoporosis landed her in the hospital more frequently than Dad's own illnesses, and her chair was replaced with a hospital bed whenever she returned from the rehabilitation center where she received her physical therapy. But she couldn't reach the TV dial, so Dad carved a slit into one end of the broomstick that fit over the raised edge of the channel dial. This way, Gam could change the channel simply by rotating the broomstick one way or the other. We could walk across the room and change it ourselves, but it was so much cooler to be in possession of the broomstick.

My aunt Liz, who usually spent her weekends at the House, often joined us. She and Dad sat together on the love seat by the bay window, separated by the gigantic bowl of popcorn Liz always prepared.

Sometimes my grandfather stepped into the room, but instead of taking his usual place on his love seat by the door, he stood there, hands in the pockets of his suit trousers, bouncing up on the balls of his feet and whistling. He was annoyed at having been displaced, but, though he never joined us, he didn't kick us out, either.

As soon as Liz saw him, she jumped up, crying, "Oh, Poppy, Poppy!" She grabbed his arm with both hands and asked, "Can I get you anything?" My grandfather stood passively, ignoring her, as if she weren't even there.

"Poppy?" There was an undercurrent of unrequited longing so deep that even I, at five years old, noticed it. Liz stood on the tips of her toes and strained to kiss her father's cheek. I had never seen my grandfather do anything physical—he didn't play sports, he didn't exercise—but he was very strongly and solidly built. In one swift movement, he spun away from his younger daughter, disentangling himself from her grasp, and left us to the movie while he returned to the glass dining table in the breakfast room to read his newspapers.

This was so different from the gentleness with which my father treated his little sister. Fred clearly had as little interest in his middle child as he had in his oldest son—or me or my brother, for that matter.

As I grew older, our only interactions, apart from our formal greetings (a handshake, a quick kiss on the cheek, "How's school?" "Fine." "Getting As?" "Yes."), were those in which my grandfather offered to buy my hair. I don't think my grandfather had had a full head of hair since he was a teenager, and he regretted his receding hairline. Both my brother and I had thick blond hair. My brother's hair was almost white blond, but mine had the advantage of being long, and we both got the same offer. It took a while for me to figure out that my grandfather didn't really have anything else to say to me, and I suppose I was happy for the attention. This became something of a ritual and I came to expect it, never taking him seriously, until he started taking his wallet out of his pocket to show me the thick wad of hundred-dollar bills he kept in it.

"I don't think it works that way, Grandpa."

18

Dad's new apartment was in the basement of a town house in Sunnyside, Queens, about twenty minutes from Jamaica without traffic.

The first time Fritz and I walked through the front door at the bottom of the cement stairs, we saw tucked in the corner of the small foyer a tank holding two garter snakes and a terrarium with a ball python named Peter. Farther along the wall that divided the foyer from the main room stood another tank, stocked with goldfish, and another with a few mice scrambling around in the straw. At first, I thought the mice and goldfish were pets, too—and then Dad explained their purpose to me.

In addition to a foldout couch, and a small refrigerator and hot plate that had been set up as a makeshift kitchen (there was no stove), Dad had furnished his new studio apartment with a card table and a couple of molded plastic chairs. Two more terrariums bookended the TV, which sat on a low shelf across from the couch. One housed an iguana named Izzy and the other a tortoise named Tomato. Dad seemed proud of his new place, with its drop ceiling and fluorescent lighting and thrift-store furniture. At the age of thirty-two, it was the first time he'd lived alone.

Staying with Dad back then was almost like being at a sleepover. At home Fritz's bedroom was at the opposite end of the apartment from mine, which could be lonely late at night when I had trouble sleeping. At Dad's place, Fritz and I shared the sofa bed and Dad slept in a sleeping bag on the floor next to us. I liked that we were all together, and Dad let us eat whatever we wanted. In the evenings, after we unfolded the sofa bed, we put Tomato on a piece of cardboard with a hunk of lettuce for her to snack on, and Izzy perched on my leg. Dad made Jiffy Pop, and after we settled in, we watched *All in the Family* and reruns of *The Twilight Zone* and *The Honeymooners*. We had no curfew, and sometimes we kept the TV on after Dad turned off the lights; when the shows were over the white noise came on.

Over the next few months, Dad taught me how to hold Peter, which made me a bit nervous at first because he was longer than I was tall. I became adept at catching the mice and goldfish and offering them up as the snakes' lunch.

Almost every other weekend there was a new addition—an earth snake named Edith (after Edith Bunker); Cornelius the corn snake, because originality in the art of naming was not our strong suit; and a boa constrictor named Baby Benjamin, who was given to me for my sixth birthday.

"It's through here," Dad said, getting ready to open the door to the boiler room just down the short dark hallway from his apartment. I hesitated, because we'd been told by the landlord that the boiler room was off limits. "Close your eyes." He ushered me through, and placed his hands on my shoulders when we reached our destination. "OK, open."

A crumpled cardboard box sat on the floor next to the boiler. A couple of heat lamps had been clipped to a wooden crate that shone down on the box's contents—six ducklings that were so small they couldn't have hatched more than a couple of days earlier.

Dad had found them out east on the way home from one of his trips to Montauk, where he still occasionally went deep-sea fishing with friends from the days when he and Mom rented the cottage. Not as often, he'd take Fritz and me out for the day. His boats were long gone, but he still knew people to charter a boat and rent rods and tackle from.

We usually started our trips at three in the morning. Dad kept the driver's-side window wide open to keep himself awake, a cigarette held loosely in his left hand. When he was relaxed, Dad was casual and confident in his movements, and I watched him from the back seat as he smoked, surveying the landscape as the day dawned, lost in thought.

The sun was up by the time we got to the Big Duck, a duck-shaped building on a dusty patch of dirt by the side of the road in a town right before Long Island split into its north and south forks. Dad pulled over. The Big Duck, which sold local produce—and ducks and duck eggs—was closed that early. We only stopped because, if the weather was good, Dad let me drive. The roads were empty and there was nothing on either side of the road but duck farms and potato and corn fields. I climbed from the back seat onto his lap, his long legs bent at an angle to make room for me. He placed my hands on the steering wheel at 10 and 2, keeping the index and middle fingers of his right hand in light contact at 6 just in case.

On his most recent solo trip, he was late getting back, so the Big Duck was deserted, but he'd pulled over to stretch his legs and saw the cardboard box, the six ducklings inside, not far from the side of the road. He didn't understand "what kind of idiot" would leave them there after the place was already closed—they would never have survived the night.

He put the box in the passenger seat, grabbed a blanket from the trunk to line the box with, and cranked the heat the rest of the way back to the basement in Sunnyside.

They were so tiny that we had to feed them sugar water with an eyedropper. Despite the landlord's prohibition against our being in the boiler room, his son, Steve, a burly guy with a thick dark beard and mustache, made allowances once the ducklings arrived. The whole room was suffused with the warm smell of the ducklings' down, straw, and mash.

I knew we wouldn't be able to keep the ducklings forever; not even the incredibly tolerant landlord, who didn't seem to mind the reptiles and mice, would put up with six grown ducks waddling around the basement—and it wouldn't be good for them anyway. I thought we'd have more time to make sure they got stronger before we found somewhere for them to live. But when we arrived the next weekend that we were scheduled to stay with Dad, everything was gone—the pets, the furniture, the hot plate. Mom had only brought us by to pick up any clothes or board games we might have left behind. She told us Dad was sick and would be away for a while. After he returned, he'd need to live in the House for a few months, so it didn't make any sense to keep the apartment.

My mother had a horrible fear of snakes, so there was no way she'd let us bring them to the Highlander, even temporarily, though we probably could have convinced her to let us keep Izzy and Tomato. But we weren't given the option.

I worried about the snakes—Peter was so gentle; Ben was sensitive and had to be handled in a particular way or he'd bite; Cornelius, sharp and lethal looking, was sweet in his own way but couldn't be held for more than a few minutes at a time. I worried about Izzy, who, like Cornelius, needed to be kept warm; I worried nobody would make the effort to give the ducklings, especially Blacky, the runt, their sugar with an eyedropper. Who would keep them warm? Mostly, I feared that my grandfather had instructed the landlord to set them all loose on the streets of Sunnyside and none of them would survive.

19

When I was four, I got a bad case of croup that worried my mother enough for her to call my father. In the immediate aftermath of the previous year's gun incident (which is how I've thought of it since, as if it were something I'd watched on an episode of *The Mod Squad*), Mom had avoided Dad as much as possible, but in the intervening year, my parents had reached a détente.

Dad was sober the night I came down with the croup, and as he sat on my bed holding me in his arms while my mother called the doctor, he teased me about the bizarre cough—a cross between a dog's bark and a horse's neigh—that was unlike any sound that should be coming out of a little girl.

"Is that a hyena?" he teased, eyes wide with mock horror. I started to laugh, but that triggered another bout of coughing. He put his palm against my chest and soothed me. Something had clearly alarmed him—perhaps the lingering rattle in my chest—because he picked me up and carried me to the kitchen, where my mother stood talking on the phone.

I ended up staying in the hospital for four days, lying in a bed draped with an oxygen tent (which I thought was very cool). The experience couldn't have been that bad—I wasn't frightened and I felt taken care of—because the worst thing I remember was the cough medicine they forced me to take, a thick, corrosive-looking chartreuse syrup with a flavor so vile I can still taste it.

I had my first asthma attack a few months later.

The experience of waking up in the early-morning darkness struggling to breathe was both disorienting and frightening. At only five years old I didn't know how to make sense of the unfamiliar sensation of not being able to breathe. When I had croup, the cough had woken me up—this was quieter and felt dangerous. The frightening unknown propelled me out of bed to my mother. Her room was adjacent to mine, and as I reached for the sleeve of her nightgown, I was wholly unaware of the implications of what I was setting in motion.

"Mom," I said, my voice barely above a whisper. She was a heavy sleeper, probably because of the depression she'd been experiencing at least since Dad left. My words failed to wake her, so with great effort, I tugged on her sleeve again.

"Mom," I repeated as she blinked her eyes open, "I can't breathe." I didn't know what was supposed to happen next, so when she said, "OK, get in," I did as I was told. I walked the long way around to the other side of her bed, slightly hunched over, as she reached across and drew down the comforter.

Her bed was high off the ground. By the time I'd climbed up next to her and pulled the comforter over my legs, she'd already turned on her side, her back to me. I don't know if she was asleep, but her breathing was even, unlike mine.

The comforter pressed heavily against me as I struggled to sit upright, instinctively knowing that this would take some pressure off my lungs. I couldn't sleep because the effort to breathe took all my focus. The entire universe collapsed down to the space between my breaths. The sum total of me became the struggle to breathe.

My mother's room was much larger than mine and occupied the southeast corner of the apartment. The bed was set far back from the windows, so the view of South Jamaica was slightly truncated compared to mine, creating a dark, lonely space, which she'd partially filled with an armchair, a small round table her father had assembled out of three pieces of intersecting plywood, and a floor lamp that, on those rare occasions it was lit, gave off a melancholy glow. Between the distance from the windows and my line of sight, I couldn't see the moon, which, on the nights it was visible, kept me company when I was in my own bed. It felt lonelier. I missed the light, but not being able to see the moon also meant I had no way to keep track of time.

The sun rose, the clock struck seven. My mother woke to find that I hadn't moved and my breathing, ragged and shallow, had worsened, coming in protracted intervals. Every single muscle in my body was tensed with the effort of inhaling, my lips thin and blue from oxygen deprivation. She got dressed while I sat on the edge of the bed and waited, my fists pressed into the mattress to reduce the pressure of gravity.

Queens General Hospital was a five-minute drive north along 164th Street, but that was not our destination. Mom passed right by it and drove for another fifteen minutes until we got to Booth Memorial Hospital, the Salvation Army hospital where she volunteered for the Women's Auxiliary and my grandfather was on the board. For years, I thought we *had* to go to Booth, not realizing that the emergency room at Queens was a perfectly good option—and it would have saved me the extra fifteen minutes on the edge of suffocation.

This visit to the hospital was different from the first one. I received a shot of epinephrine, and then another when the first failed to break through. And then another. When my condition failed to improve after an hour or two, the doctor ordered an IV with a fluid drip of prednisone. The needle, sliding into my small vein, hurt in a new way, but I barely noticed. My progress was so slow, the doctors decided I needed to be admitted.

They wheeled me to the children's ward and put me in a room with four beds, two of which were already occupied. Dim lights at the head of each bed were lit, and the flare of the fluorescents flooded in from the hallway, along with the occasional screams of the other patients. One of my roommates was asleep, but the other kept up a steady moan, whether from pain or homesickness I didn't know. A nurse came in every hour or so to take my vital signs, but I wouldn't have been able to sleep anyway—I was exhausted but also shaky and wired; the epinephrine had speeded up my heart rate and saddled me with a massive headache. My heart pounded hard against my chest. Many hours passed before I felt any significant relief. In order to find out if my lungs were drawing enough oxygen as well as exhaling enough carbon dioxide, the doctor had to take arterial-blood-gas measurements from an artery in my wrist, introducing me to an entirely new class of pain.

After I got home, I had to continue taking oral steroids plus theophylline, a long-acting drug that helped reduce the tightness in my chest by relaxing the bronchial muscles. It also stripped all of the potassium out of my body. Finally back in my bed and able to sleep uninterrupted—without crying roommates or a nurse taking my temperature, pulse, and blood pressure seemingly every time I was about to nod off—I woke up in the middle of the night with charley horses so intense I thought my calves were going to explode. My doctors then prescribed a liquid potassium supplement that tasted so awful, nothing I mixed with it could mask the taste. The cramps almost seemed a reasonable alternative.

The next time I woke up with that awful weight on my chest, I went to my mother as quickly as possible. After tugging her awake, I whispered, "Mom, I think I need to go to the hospital." All I needed to do was ask, I thought. But asking changed nothing.

"OK, get in," she said, still half-asleep.

The sky too dark for hope, the sleepless wait commenced. I exhaled as slowly as I could—although it was less an exhalation than a dread-filled surrender. Because what would happen next? I was beginning to understand that there was no guarantee I would be able to refill my lungs. The hours of waiting became one long seamless struggle to engage in the function most basic to sustaining life while every other aspect of what it means to be human was fractured and then obliterated. This moment, in the interstice between exhaling and inhaling, stretched into an eternity that was a cold, black emptiness accompanied by the sound of life bleeding out of me.

The sun rose; the clock struck seven.

Next time, I tried another tack, a declarative statement with no qualifications: "Mom, I need to go to the hospital."

"OK, get in."

Five or six hours later, my muscles tight with the labor of breathing, lips blue from oxygen deprivation, the sun rose; the clock struck seven.

By the time I was six, I'd been to the hospital—and admitted—at least four or five times. Almost every experience I had during the first year or two after I started having asthma attacks introduced a new, unexpected, and unavoidable pain—sometimes specific and acute, sometimes more diffuse. Making it all the more difficult was the unfamiliar sensation of being pinned down. I had always moved so easily through the world, like liquid, unburdened.

Asthma almost always strikes at 1:00 or 2:00 A.M., when we're supine and when, during sleep, our airways narrow, increasing airflow resistance. It also didn't help that I was severely allergic to our cat, who often slept next to me. I'd learned through all those visits to the emergency room that serious asthma attacks, in the days before the rescue inhaler was invented, had to be treated immediately.

Sometimes it wouldn't be until the evening of the second or third day that my breathing improved enough for me to feel less afraid of suffocating, and for that blood-gas needle to become the next thing I dreaded most. I usually got released from the hospital after four or five days, depending on how bad things had gotten—how close the call. By then my breathing was fine, but my body was battered. The intensity of the effort to breathe combined with the quantity and strength of the drugs exhausted me.

When the doctor discharged me, my lungs were clear, but I hadn't slept or eaten properly in days and I wanted to go home right away. Instead, after picking me up from my room and packing up my stuff, Mom took me to another wing of the hospital, where the Women's Auxiliary had its headquarters. She told me she needed to pick up some paperwork on the way to the car, but instead, she stopped in every office and at every desk to talk to whoever was there.

"Mary's just getting out of the hospital again."

"Oh, no. Linda!"

I stayed by her side, quiet, trying to stand upright, but leaning against the wall when there was one nearby. I didn't want to be rude, but I also didn't have the energy to engage. She got her attention, she got her sympathy. And that was the point.

I learned to adjust my expectations. I became expert at waiting, a study of patience in extremis. I waited past endurance; I waited long after agony set in. Maybe if it gets bad enough—if she sees how bad it is—she'll take me to the hospital right away. When it got to the point that inhaling felt like trying to draw air through a narrow, partially obstructed straw, I swung my legs slowly over the edge of my bed. It took much longer to get to my mother's room now. I shuffled my feet, hunched over like an old woman, stopping at intervals, my palms pressed against my thighs in an effort to relieve the tension on my upper back. When I reached her bedside, I didn't have the ability to speak. I tapped her on the shoulder and waited for her to open her eyes. When she did, I stood there, bent over, my shoulders pulled forward, barely able to keep my head up, and waited. She took one look at me.

"OK, get in."

The seed of the knowledge had been planted: the worst way to be alone is to be alone in the presence of the one person who is supposed to love you most, protect you most, but who decides instead to turn her back on you and fall asleep. I sat up against the pillows, every muscle tensed with effort. I could not move, but there was no stillness. Next to me, she slept, her breathing shallow, steady, and rhythmic. It was the loneliest sound.

PART II

Black Velocities

I do what many dream of, all their lives,
—Dream? strive to do, and agonize to do,
And fail in doing.

—ROBERT BROWNING, "Andrea del Sarto"

20

1971

Cabin 1 was farther from the camp entrance than any other cabin, in a clearing by the sandy footpath to the beach. Families, cars, and campers with their trunks were everywhere. After Mom dropped me off, one of my counselors took me inside. It was a relief to be out of the sun and away from the commotion of the farewells and reunions.

My trunk had been set down next to one of the bunk beds to the right of the door. My brother had taken Dad's National Guard trunk, so I inherited the trunk my uncle Rob had used for summer camp. By the time it came into my possession, it was probably fifteen years old, and so solidly built that it lasted me another thirteen years. Rob had drawn his initials—RST—with white paint in huge block letters in the top left corner of the trunk's lid. I wrote my initials in smaller letters in the lower right. I sat down on it, feeling unsure for the first time.

The counselor, who seemed very old but couldn't have been much more than eighteen, had a HELLO MY NAME IS CORY sticker attached to her camp shirt. "Do you want the top bunk?" she asked.

"I guess," I said. I didn't know if that's what I wanted—I'd never been on a bunk bed before.

She patted the mattress. I clambered up. My feet dangled over the edge; it was so high up and far away from everything that I started to feel a little bit afraid.

"What do you think?" she asked.

I tried to smile.

"OK, Trump." She grabbed me under the shoulders, lifted me up, and swung me gently onto the floor. "Let's get you unpacked."

The next morning, I discovered I hadn't packed a hairbrush, but I was afraid to say anything. My hair was long and thick and knotted easily—especially after I washed it. I'd gotten used to walking around with knots so large I couldn't get an elastic band around a ponytail. At home, after I showered, my mother sometimes sat me on a low-backed chair with a towel wrapped around my shoulders and alternated between spraying detangler in my hair and trying to tease out the knots with a comb. She usually gave up long before the problem had been solved. "This is impossible," she'd say. I heard the phrase "rat's nest" more than any child should.

On a trip out to California one summer, we stayed with a friend of hers who offered to try to get the knots out for me. "Her hair is like yarn," my mother said casually, as if this explained anything. "You pull it and it just snaps back and tangles." The detangling took an hour and a half, the two women chatting away the whole time.

It didn't matter so much when I wasn't in school, and somehow my hair always managed to be smooth and shiny and knot-free when we went to the House, otherwise I doubt my grandfather would have offered to buy it. I didn't have any self-consciousness about it. My mother, an impeccably groomed woman who got her nails and hair done once a week, didn't, either.

But this was different. At camp we were supposed to be able to take care of ourselves—whether that meant organizing our laundry, making our beds, or brushing our own hair.

Over the course of the previous year, I had set out the case for my being allowed to go to sleepaway camp very logically, at least in my mind. I listed all the reasons it would be good for me to be away for eight weeks the summer before first grade. I also explained why, even though I was only six and the camp didn't admit campers younger than seven, I was mature enough—ready enough—for an exception to be made.

My "lobbying," the word subsequently used to describe my efforts, succeeded, although I think my logic had nothing to do with the decision. My mother wanted a break, and she probably agreed with me that I'd be better off at a sailing camp on Cape Cod Bay than playing hopscotch and freeze tag in Jamaica parking lots for another summer. The people in charge of the camp didn't care either way. My brother, Fritz, and cousin David were already campers, so they knew the family—and they knew who Fred Trump was.

Whatever the case, I needed to prove that they hadn't made a mistake by letting me come a year early. Having knots in my hair would not help me make that case, so I hid them, at first by smoothing the outer layer of my hair over them and then, when that became impossible, by pulling my hair back in a ponytail. That soon became impossible as well when my elastic bands were stretched past their breaking point.

One morning, I stayed back from breakfast—which was not allowed. I knew I would get in trouble, but I was willing to risk it because I worried more about somebody finding out about the knots; if they did, I was sure they'd send me home. After taking a comb from one of my cabin mates, I sat on my bunk and tried to work it through my hair, but it didn't budge. It was, as my mother said, impossible.

Someone came into the cabin, and I endeavored to hide in the corner so I wouldn't be caught. Maybe if I missed my morning activities and figured out how to get one knot out at a time, I could make enough progress by lunchtime at least to manage a ponytail again. I pushed myself against the wooden partition separating my side of the cabin from the entryway in hopes that whoever it was wouldn't see me. But it was me Cory was looking for.

"There you are! We've been worried about you." She seemed relieved, not angry. Maybe I wasn't in trouble after all. "What's the matter?" I didn't say anything. She saw the comb in my hand. It had a name tag on it, so she knew immediately I'd taken it. "Come here, kiddo." She grabbed my ankles gently and pulled me toward the edge of my bunk. Under different circumstances, this would have made me laugh. She asked me to turn my head and didn't say anything right away, as if she were working something out. My cheeks burned with the same feeling I'd had when that girl's mother slapped me across the face and Mrs. Lombardi spanked me, but I wasn't sure why. I braced myself.

"OK, Trump. I've got an idea. Come with me."

I didn't move. I was afraid to ask the question, but not knowing where we were going was even worse. I swallowed hard and hoped I wouldn't start to cry. "Can I stay?" I asked almost in a whisper.

Cory looked confused. "Stay in the cabin?"

"No," I forced myself to say. "At camp."

"Don't be silly," she said with a laugh, lifting me down from my bunk as she'd done on the first day. "We just need some help."

The infirmary was a small square building set back from the dirt road that marked the camp's property line. After Cory dropped me off, the nurse, a tall woman with broad shoulders and a gruff manner, took me into one of the exam rooms, which also doubled as a bedroom for campers who were too sick to sleep in the cabin. She put on a pair of exam gloves and examined my hair and scalp with a fine-tooth metal comb with a long, pointed handle. "No lice," she announced. I didn't know what lice were, but she seemed pleased.

"Now, for this." For the next hour she peppered me with questions about my health (she seemed particularly interested in my visits to the hospital), my interests, and what I liked about camp, while she expertly untangled my hair strand by strand. Since realizing I was going to be allowed to stay, I had returned to my normally loquacious self. I had already become adept at staying still and withstanding pain, and I barely noticed the time or the hair-pulling.

When she finished, she ran a brush through my hair again, took an elastic out of her pocket, and swept my hair up in a bun. She told me to wait and stepped out of the room. When she came back, she handed me an envelope and told me to give it to Cory.

Before I left, she rested her large hand on top of my head. "Two things before you go: One, do you know how to get knots out of your hair?"

I shook my head beneath the weight of her hand.

"Two: Ask your counselors for help. Got it?"

"Got it."

"Trump," she shouted as I opened the door. "Three things!" I ducked back inside and she threw me a lollipop.

Once we campers settled into our respective cabins to get ready for bed, the loudspeakers, nailed high up in pine trees throughout camp, crackled as if a needle were being placed on a record. When a camper had a visitor or a phone call, somebody in the office called over the PA system the name and where the kid needed to go. At night, a bugle played a slow, mournful tune I later learned was called taps. The next morning, the same bugle played reveille to wake us.

Camp revealed itself to be a highly organized place that relied heavily on routine and tradition. After breakfast, we were each assigned a chore, cleaning the bathrooms or sweeping the floor, in addition to making our beds and putting our clothes away. In the center of each unit, four ten-foot-long pine planks resting on cinder blocks had been arranged in a square, and this "council ring" was where we met to pick our activities for the day. The outside world did not intrude. It was 1971, yet there was no indication that the Vietnam War raged, or that young adults across the country—the same age as most of the counselors— were protesting the senseless conflict or being sent to fight in it.

At six I was only dimly aware of this and wouldn't have understood why some people might have found the conservative, quasi-militaristic atmosphere offensive. None of the campers or counselors looked like the kids back home with their long hair, cigarettes, army jackets with POW/MIA patches, tie-dye, and bell-bottoms. Cape Cod was not Queens, and the Cape Cod Sea Camps were not Jamaica.

I liked wearing the uniform—forest-green shorts, white T-shirt with green trim and the camp logo, and, on occasion, a matching hat. I liked the fact that every evening before dinner we marched in formation to the parade grounds—a flat expanse of green lawn that stretched across the middle of the camp—to lower the American flag. We stood at attention, organized by units, around the flagpole and saluted. Every day each unit selected a different camper as its representative in the color guard, which was considered an honor. The highest honor, though, was being chosen to fold the flag, which we were taught to do with military precision.

The powers that be paced our days perfectly—two activity periods in the morning and two in the afternoon, separated by lunch and a rest period, which we had to spend on our beds whether we were napping, reading, or writing letters. Everything was organized—from the way we did laundry to the way we lined up for meals. I had never known such order, structure, or discipline before. The routine and the expectations helped me make sense of the world. To know when I needed to do what and where I wanted to be; to know what the rules were and what would happen if I broke them—all of this made me feel safe.

A few times a summer there were optional off-campus activities—a Red Sox game at Fenway, deep-sea fishing—which were a little more free-wheeling. That first summer I signed up for a day trip to Nantucket. By the time the ferry pulled out of the harbor in Hyannis, ominous storm clouds had gathered and strong gusts of wind whipped the sea into a frenzy. Halfway across Nantucket Sound it started to pour. Most people huddled in the cramped and stifling cabin, but I stayed on the deck with a couple of other campers as seawater poured across the bow. One rogue wave and we would have been swept out to sea, but we arrived at Brant's Point intact and exhilarated—and soaking wet.

One of our counselors brought us first to a souvenir shop, where she bought a few cheap beach towels, and then to a laundromat just off the main street. She had us strip to our underwear, wrapped us in the towels, and sat us on top of the dryers as our clothes dried within them.

I think this was similar to my father's appreciation of ROTC in college, but we came at it from different vantage points. My parents weren't disciplinarians, partly because they didn't need to be, but mostly because they didn't know how to be. My grandfather, on the other hand, was very strict, but his rules followed a logic apparent only to him. Whereas my parents rarely knew what I was doing and had only the vaguest notion of where I was most of the time, my grandfather overwhelmed his oldest son with expectations. Freddy, in Fred's mind at least, needed to be a killer; in order to create that drive in him, Fred had tried deprivation, punishment, and unrelenting criticism.

It turns out Dad and I craved the same thing—the discipline and order that ROTC and flying, for him, and camp, for me, brought to our lives. If you work hard to improve your skills, you're rewarded. In both my grandfather's house and in his business, Dad was never rewarded for anything he did, because he was simply expected to do everything according to specification. There was no such thing as exceeding expectations because they could never be met—a shell game Fred would never play with his middle son, Donald.

Almost an entire week passed after my arrival before I got to see my brother for the first time. Every Sunday, the girls' camp—campers and counselors—walked the half mile along the beach to Monomoy for vespers, a pseudo-religious service, which was presented by a different unit every week at the outdoor amphitheater and consisted of songs, recitations, and award presentations.

Vespers would become a highlight of my week, but that first time, all I cared about was seeing Fritz. As soon as my unit left the beach and walked up the hill toward the theater, I started looking for him.

When I finally spotted him with a few other boys, loping along, tall and skinny like my father, I wanted to run over and throw myself in his arms. With the exception of my first night in Cabin 1, I hadn't been homesick until I saw his shock of white-blond hair in the distance.

"Hey," he said when I finally reached him. I waited for permission to hug him, but he didn't move any closer to me. He shook his too-long hair out of his eyes and kept his hands in his pockets.

"Hey," I said back to him.

It took me a few seconds to realize that that was going to be it. My eyes stung with tears as he walked away with his friends, tossing a casual "See ya" over his shoulder. But I didn't cry. And I was never homesick again.

I was never bored or lonely at home, but living in a cabin with sixteen other people made it easier to get close quickly and learn how to tolerate other people. Even with kids who were much older and counselors, there was a sense of solidarity. I was connected to people in an entirely new way.

Three times a day, the entire camp convened in the cavernous dining hall amid a cacophony of plates and flatware and chairs scraping against the wooden floor, and at any moment, somebody could break into song, soon joined by the rest of the people at their table and then their whole unit. The dining hall erupted in an impromptu singing competition, with each unit shouting its own song at the top of its collective lungs, complete with foot-stomping and table-slamming. Sometimes we'd all suddenly be on the same page, as if a signal had been sent, with hundreds of voices raised in the same melody.

Oh, it's gin gin gin
That makes you want to sin
In the corps
In the corps

The song could have gone on forever—gin replaced by wine, wine by beer—but when somebody shouted out "ice-cold duck" we got shut down before we could get to the rhyme.

There was a joyousness and spontaneity that complemented our usual routine. We sang in our cabins and council rings; we sang in small groups or with the entire camp harmonizing, every voice somehow finding its place.

21

When you're six or twelve or even sixteen, you never think: I'm wasting my time, or This will never amount to anything. You dive in. And I did, like a kid at a banquet who hadn't realized she was starving. I tried everything and loved all of it, even things I wasn't particularly good at, like woodworking, as long as there was the possibility I could get better, and stayed away from things for which I had no talent or affinity, like art and Ultimate Frisbee. In the same week I could shoot a bow and arrow or a .22, play tennis, go canoeing, and perform in a play.

I discovered that I was an athlete, and I was good at almost every sport I tried, most of which, like archery and sailing, I'd never encountered before. I arrived at camp a proficient swimmer, but we swam in the bay every day, unless there was lightning, and I became an incredibly strong one. This opened up an entirely new world to me not just of skill and achievement, but of competition. I wanted to be better than other people, but more than anything, I just wanted to be better. I'd been on motorboats Dad piloted, from small twelve-foot outboards to a forty-foot Chris-Craft, since before I could remember, but I'd never been on a sailboat. The steering felt familiar because the tiller on a sailboat works the same way as the little outboard on our Boston Whaler did. But how did the sails work?

Camp had a fleet of twenty Mercuries, fifteen-foot sloops with a mainsail and a jib, but little kids were consigned to dinghies, which didn't appeal to me. They were shaped like dumpy oval bathtubs, undecked, with very thin gunwales, which left us sitting in puddles of salty water and sand, the cause for innumerable cases of butt rash. But the sailing counselors taught us the parts of the boat and sails; the terms for all of the equipment; the positions of the bow in relation to wind direction; and how to read a racecourse (even dinghies had regattas every Sunday).

On really windy days, dinghies were grounded because they didn't handle well in heavy weather. So we sat on the beach and watched the older kids, hulls tilting out of the water, decks nearly perpendicular to the sea.

I desperately wanted to sail a Merc, but I was too small to skipper, and too weak, especially on a day with a decent amount of wind, to hold the sheet of even the smaller sail. In subsequent years, as I got older, they let me serve as second crew, as long as the wind wasn't too strong, mostly to serve as ballast or to catch the block for the mooring. Even though there wasn't much for me to do, I always learned something, from trimming a sail properly to finding pockets of breeze on calm days that created dark patches of small, choppy waves, which, if you hit them just right, would fill the sails and lift the bow into the wind.

Mom visited us once or twice a summer. The three of us would spend a day at a beach on the ocean side of the Cape, or shopping in Orleans for blueberry muffins or saltwater taffy to bring back to the cabin. At night we went out to dinner.

Dad visited a few times during those early years as well, but he never seemed comfortable on the Cape, and he never knew what to do with us, which, considering we were surrounded by water, didn't make any sense. Sometimes we drove aimlessly around as if he hoped we'd stumble on something to do. It was as if he were fulfilling an obligation he wasn't up to.

After a lunch at Land Ho! spent almost entirely in silence, we stopped at the army and navy store in town and picked up an inflatable canvas rowboat. We took it down to Skaket Beach, just down the road from his motel, but Dad had forgotten to buy a pump. Fritz and I splashed around in the shallows while Dad, sitting in the sand wearing khakis rolled up to his knees and a white T-shirt, spent almost an hour blowing the boat up with nothing but the air from his two-pack-a-day lungs. The tide was going out. When the boat was finally ready—only half-inflated but with enough air in it to stay afloat with us on board—the water between sandbars only reached to his knees and he had to bend over to push us along (he'd forgotten oars and a towline as well).

The last time Dad visited, I was nine or ten, and he seemed OK. He took us to a clam shack about a mile from camp for steamers and lobster. When we got back, Fritz needed to get back to his unit, so Dad and I walked down to the beach. I told him how much I loved sailing, how excited I was to be allowed on Mercs once in a while, and how different the experience was from the boats we chartered out of Montauk.

We sat on the edge of the sea, the tide as high as it was going to get. Dad lit a cigarette as a little prop plane towing a banner passed by. Dad identified it as the same kind of plane he rented to fly to Montauk when he first started working at Trump Management. I dug in the sand around me in search of flat stones, and skipped them into the incoming waves.

He placed his hand over his eyes and peered across the water. "How long has that been there?" he asked, pointing to the old decommissioned battleship that was anchored in the middle of the bay.

"The target ship? Oh, forever, I guess." I meant it had been there since I first came to the Cape. But it had been there since 1945 and was used for target practice until 1970.

Its silhouette was a fixture of the seascape of my childhood, but every summer there was less of it as the wind and salt water ate away at the hull until finally it split in half and eventually disappeared entirely.

Dad liked the idea of navy jets spraying the rusting hulk of the target ship with missiles.

Looking out at the Mercs that were tacking and jibing around anchored buoys, sailing downwind and close-hauled, Dad said it was a lot like piloting a motorboat or a plane. All of them involved a constant recalibration. I told him about trimming sails. If you point the bow too close to the wind or pull the sail too tight, it pinches, letting wind slip away. If you let the sails out too far, they begin to flap, or luff, wasting surface area. Wind is rarely steady, and the position of the bow in relation to the wind is always changing, so you're always making small adjustments to the sails and the rudder.

We watched for a while in silence. Dad looked at his watch and lit another cigarette.

"I have an idea. Let me make a couple of phone calls and I'll find a place to rent a boat." He pointed across the bay to Provincetown. The lighthouse gleamed amber in the afternoon sun. "I'll come before lunch tomorrow. If we leave from a marina in Dennis we can head to Provincetown and check out the battleships and the lighthouse, then maybe find a mooring in the harbor and grab a lobster roll." I smiled at him—we'd be back on familiar territory again. And maybe he'd be transformed.

By lunchtime, I hadn't been called up to the office yet. My counselor let me stay back at the unit so I could hear the announcement. But that wouldn't come for another hour. When it did, I walked to the office instead of running because I knew Dad wasn't going to be there.

"Your father won't be coming," Ginny, the woman behind the front desk, with a huge bouffant and wearing a brightly patterned muumuu, told me. "He got called back to New York unexpectedly." I'd known Ginny since my brother's first summer at camp, and she always did her best to make the lie sound convincing.

She usually failed, as she did this time, and I thought briefly that there wasn't anybody in New York who wanted him. When I got back to my cabin, I was angry with myself for actually believing Dad. But at least I didn't have to hear my mother tell me what a miserable failure he was, how much she hated him.

Dad had done this before. Sometimes we were told he was coming up and he didn't show. Or, if it was clear to the staff that he'd been drinking, whoever was manning the desk in the office, usually Ginny, sent him away and told us he wasn't feeling well enough to see us. Before he left, he sometimes asked if he could cash a check. These always bounced. When they called my grandfather to cover it, he told them to put it on his tab.

That evening I was back in my unit, winding down from the day with my friends. They asked me how the visit with Dad went, but I just shrugged and said he'd had to cancel. They'd heard it before. It wasn't worth discussing. The scratch of the PA crackled over the loudspeakers, but it was too early for taps. Then the voice of one of the camp directors came on. He told us we all needed to head to the bay immediately. "You don't want to miss tonight's sunset," he said.

We stopped what we were doing and took the pathway that lay between the riflery range and tennis courts and went past the swimming pool. Camp was the first place I'd ever been in my life where natural beauty was treated as something worth paying attention to, as something that was valuable in its own right.

The tide was out, and we walked straight into the empty basin of the bay as the horizon darkened in the east and the sky in the west turned from blue and pink to purple and flame orange. The colors lit up the clouds and reflected off the tide pools, like artists' palettes that had been scattered across the flats. We walked with our arms slung around each other's shoulders in quiet solidarity, hushed by the beauty that hovered above us with the magnificence of a cathedral.

22

We had two or three weeks after getting home from camp to get ready for school, which started later than public school. In between shopping for our uniforms and school supplies, we spent days at the Belcrest pool or North Shore beaches; I met my friends in the parking lot for our usual games, but a summer away had created some distance between me and them. After we'd learned how to sail and shoot archery, our games of red light, green light and hide-and-seek had lost some of their charm.

Trump Management owned box seats a few rows up from the first-base line at Shea Stadium, home to the New York Mets, my favorite team. In the late sixties, my grandfather used them to curry favor with business associates or as sops to his cronies, but in the two years since winning the 1969 World Series, the Mets had made a long, quick slide and were widely considered the worst in baseball. Tickets had gotten harder to give away, so my grandmother gave us the leftovers, of which there were plenty.

There were a lot more day games back then, so on a random weekday Fritz and I, sometimes with Mom or Dad, sometimes on our own, took the 7 train to Flushing, baseball gloves in tow just in case a fly ball landed in our vicinity. I loved Shea. It was small and intimate—and usually more than half-empty. As the mellow summer afternoons softened gently into twilight, there was no better place to be on a late-summer day in New York, Sabrett hot dog in hand, than in a box, six rows up from the dugout.

I was excited about first grade but ambivalent about going to Kew-Forest. I had wanted to go to a school in the neighborhood, like all of my friends. Kew-Forest was a twenty-minute drive without traffic. During rush hour it could be considerably more. My parents told me the reason I couldn't go to the elementary school that was only a couple of blocks away was because it backed onto the campus of Hillcrest High School, which, they'd heard, had frequent stabbings.

Either way, my attendance at Kew-Forest was preordained, not because Fritz and my cousin David were already students and all of my aunts and uncles had been, but because my grandfather was on the board of trustees at the school. There was no choice to be made.

My grandfather's reputation preceded me. Very few people outside of New York City were familiar with the name Fred Trump, but within the five boroughs, especially Brooklyn and Queens, he was famous—a phenomenally wealthy real estate developer who probably had more money than everybody else at Kew-Forest combined. I never learned why he became a board member there. He had no interest in education and Forest Hills was far from his usual stomping grounds. Yet all of his children, except for his oldest son, went to Kew-Forest. After eight years at public school, my dad had attended St. Paul's, an all-boys private school on Long Island. Donald's time at Kew-Forest had been ignominiously cut short.

The trouble with Donald had started long before he entered school. At home, he tormented his little brother, Robert, a year and a half younger, and seemed to have nothing but disdain for everybody else, including, and perhaps especially, his mother. The kids in the neighborhood alternately despised and feared him; he had a reputation for being a thin-skinned bully who beat up on younger kids but ran home in a fit of rage as soon as somebody stood up to him.

Nobody liked Donald when he was growing up, not even his parents. As he got older, those personality traits hardened, the hostile indifference and aggressive disrespect that he'd developed as a toddler to help him withstand the neglect he suffered at his parents' hands—from his mother because she was seriously ill and psychologically unstable, and from his father because, as a sociopath, he had no interest in his children outside of Freddy, who, at least initially, was being groomed to take over his empire. Even so, the interest wasn't love—Fred Trump was incapable of loving anybody.

Donald's reputation at school also preceded me. By second grade he was already known as a troublemaker who contradicted his teachers and resorted to physical violence when he didn't get his way. He treated students who were smaller and weaker than he was, and his teachers, with the same contempt with which he treated his family. After he finished seventh grade, despite my grandfather's place on the board, the school administrators made it clear that other accommodations had to be made for Fred's obnoxious middle son.

Instead of fixing the problem, moving Donald to another school only transferred it elsewhere. At the time my father was mystified by the fact that Fred couldn't control Donald, but I suspect my grandfather didn't want to waste his time trying. He was happy to delegate the responsibility to the staff at New York Military Academy, a boarding school in central New York State that was essentially a rich kids' alternative to reform school. Everybody in the family, especially his mother, was relieved when Donald was sent away.

At camp, my brother and I, separated as we were by that half-mile stretch of beach, might as well have been on opposite

sides of the planet. At school, my brother's classroom was diagonally across the hall from mine. Everybody knew who he
was; there were only 350 students in the whole school, and
only twenty students in each of grades one through six. Fritz
was funny, athletic, and cute. Everybody loved him. Kew-
Forest was not going to be a blank slate. At camp, almost
nobody knew about my grandfather, and I was "Trump," on
my own terms, free of preconception or expectation. At school
I would be Mary, my brother's sister and, more significantly,
Fred Trump's granddaughter.

Having already been away from home for two months, I felt
little anxiety about starting school. Our teacher was sweet and
gentle, and I already knew how to read and write pretty fluently,
so I wasn't worried about the schoolwork.

But even though I loved the work, and I came to love my
friends, some of whom would remain my friends for decades,
there was always a tension in the background, aside from or
adjacent to the issues with my family (and I wouldn't understand that until much later). Even at the beginning, I felt like I
had one hand—and sometimes two—tied behind my back. My
asthma was getting worse. I missed a lot of school, and when I
returned after having been in the hospital, I often felt depleted,
with nothing to show for my time away but dark circles under my eyes. The knots in my hair continued to get bigger—or
maybe it just seemed that way because the older I got the more
self-conscious I became about them, as if they were a reflection
on me and my lack of worth.

I lost touch pretty quickly with most of my friends from Jamaica.
Fritz and I still spent most weekends at my grandparents' house,
and by the time I got home it was usually too late in the day
to hang out. Plus, two days a week I took ballet and tap at a

second-floor dance studio in South Jamaica with the daughters
of my mother's friends. I didn't mind dancing, although I had
no interest in it. I preferred ballet to tap, but I wasn't particularly
good at either, and I instinctively knew that even if I put a great
deal of effort into it, I never would be.

I didn't mind the girls, either, it's just that we had nothing
in common, something that became more obvious the older we
got. We'd been going to each other's birthday parties and hanging at the park with our mothers since we were little, but the
dance classes had less to do with nurturing our friendships and
more to do with our mothers wanting to take the adult class, and
enrolling us made that easier to justify.

I remember the adult recital number—a cancan in a speak-
easy set to "Big Spender," the women in black-and-gold cos-
tumes, complete with feather headdresses and matching boas,
mesh stockings, and high-heel tap shoes—much more clearly
than anything I did at that school for the six years we were there,
with one exception.

In order to participate in the recital, I had to wear a bun
for the ballet performance. I didn't want to. It was such a small
thing, but the more my mother insisted, the more I dug my
heels in. I didn't object to the bun because I was a tomboy. I had
been fine with it when the camp nurse had put my hair in a bun
after she'd spent so much time detangling it. I had no problem
wearing the tights, and the leotard, and the ballet slippers—
I understood uniforms and what was required to participate in a
discipline whether I was interested in it or not. And I wasn't test-
ing boundaries—I was usually a very obedient child, and though
I stuck up for myself when I felt I'd been wronged, I never talked
back.

But I drew the line at the bun, because giving in to my

mother would have felt like relinquishing control over myself when I didn't have to. The more adamantly I refused, the more she tried to force me; the more she forced me, the more adamant I got.

It meant so much to her, and she seemed so hurt by my refusal, that it made me angry. This was my first glimpse into the possibility that my mother didn't see me as a being separate from her, with my own needs and preferences. She wanted to be the child who took ballet and got to wear the bun, but since that hadn't happened, she wanted a daughter who wanted those things—and that wasn't me.

I came back from camp stronger and more coordinated, and decided I didn't need the training wheels on my bike anymore. The weekend before first grade started, Luca Lombardi removed them from my old-fashioned Raleigh, which weighed almost as much as I did. He and Teresa and I walked to the top of a hill that sloped down from the park entrance to the pond. They stood on either side of me, gripping the handlebars and back of the seat. The plan was for them to hold me until I found my balance and then give me a push in the hope that momentum and the sheer terror of falling would force me to stay upright. Fritz waited at the bottom of the hill in case I fell.

Luca's cigarette dangled from his lips. Through a cloud of smoke, he said, "OK, stay on the bike and don't crash into Fritz. Keep pedaling until you get to the bottom of the hill and then slowly step on the brakes. Otherwise, you might land in the pond."

I nodded, suddenly not feeling as brave as I had when I agreed to this. "Hey, Fritz," Luca yelled, waving to my brother. "You ready?"

Fritz gave a thumbs-up.

"Are *you* ready?" Luca asked me.

I was not ready. I nodded again.

"OK," he whispered. And they let me go.

23

Almost every Sunday, my grandfather sent his dark blue Cadillac limousine to pick my brother and me up for Sunday breakfast at the House. We waited on the sidewalk across the street from the Highlander so Ed, the chauffeur, didn't have to make a U-turn. When he pulled up to the curb, Fritz and I, dressed in our sneakers and jeans and T-shirts, jumped in.

On Saturdays, before I was old enough to join him, my brother often rode his bike to our cousin David's apartment in Jamaica Estates or to the House, where the two of them met our uncle Rob to play soccer. If my mother wasn't around to give me a ride, I got stuck at home.

I wanted to have the kind of freedom Fritz had; if I could ride to my grandparents' house under my own steam, he wouldn't so easily be able to leave me behind. But the main reason I had wanted the training wheels off my bike was so I wouldn't have to ride in my grandfather's limo anymore. If any of my neighborhood friends was around to see Ed arrive, I felt self-conscious. It embarrassed me, sitting in the back seat of that pretentious Cadillac, but also, deep down, it made me feel superior, which embarrassed me to the point of shame. And that made me feel like I didn't belong anywhere.

I spent a lot of time practicing on the two-wheeler in the flat expanse of the Belcrest parking lot or along the cement path that ringed the pond. The Raleigh, heavy and unwieldy, made it difficult to negotiate the many hills in the neighborhood, so I often ended up having to dismount when my legs gave out and the bike threatened to tip over. I probably pushed that bike more than I rode it.

I finally convinced my parents to let me trade in the Raleigh for a Schwinn, complete with sissy bar, sparkling blue banana seat, and low-slung handlebars. After that, my friends and I rode everywhere, even those places that were tacitly forbidden to us, like the road that bordered the dark, overgrown back corner of the park. We'd lean our bikes against the parking meters outside the candy store that stood in a solitary block of small businesses, drink a vanilla soda from the fountain, and then leave with a handful of Bazooka bubble gum at two for a penny before riding down the desolate street that wound past the edge of the thick stand of oak trees at the perpetually dark corner of the park across from Jamaica High School.

To get to the House, it was a straight shot down Highland Avenue until it dead-ended at Homelawn Street, the border between Jamaica and Jamaica Estates. Getting across Homelawn to Henley Road, which wound through the west part of the neighborhood all the way to Midland Parkway, the town's main thoroughfare, required taking a sharp left turn, cutting across oncoming traffic, and powering up a short, steep stretch of road before taking the right onto Henley.

My grandparents' house, a lopsided Georgian with an off-center portico held up by six massive Corinthian columns, loomed on top of another steep hill. My grandfather had a fabricated family crest and Latin motto inscribed on the pediment. Nobody knew what the motto stood for, although my father suggested it might be "Don't bullshit a bullshitter."

Every time we visited (other than Thanksgiving and Christmas, when we climbed the wide flagstone steps to the front door) we left our bikes on the driveway next to the garage door and took a narrow cement pathway to the back door.

When it wasn't raining, we played soccer or threw a baseball around, depending on which of our uncles was there. Rob was the soccer player—he'd been on Boston University's team as an undergrad. He was good and I wanted to learn from him, but, as the youngest by far and the only girl, I usually ended up being the monkey in the middle.

It didn't take long to realize that Donald couldn't do much more than throw a baseball, which he did, as hard as he could, at his niece and nephews, who were all under ten. For my eighth birthday, Fritz got me a catcher's mitt. This mitt, which looked like something a major league catcher would own, had glossy to-bacco leather and two-inch padding. Eventually, I realized he'd bought me the glove to protect my hand bones from Donald's fastball. Luckily for us, Donald usually missed his target, but when he did connect, the impact reverberated all the way up my arm. The boys were undoubtedly waiting for the day when they were old enough and strong enough to turn the tables on him, although he would, of course, stop playing catch with them long before that could happen.

I did my best to keep up, but the last straw was when Rob started using me for target practice. I loved Rob, partially be-cause he was younger and not above hanging out with us. He took us for rides in his red convertible and we went to Burger King and Nino's, the pizza place on the corner of Midland Park-way and Hillside Avenue. He also seemed the most human of them; I thought he was different.

I had a tendency to get styes when I was young, and one weekend I showed up with the worst one I'd ever had; my left eye was almost completely swollen shut. Rob joked that it would be simpler if he kicked the ball into my face to deflate it. We all laughed. When we started playing the game, Rob and I were on the same team. I waved my arms and yelled for him to pass me the ball. He stopped. I couldn't have been more than fifteen feet away, but he approached the soccer ball as if he were teeing up a thirty-yard penalty kick. When his foot made contact with the ball, it sounded like a thunderclap. The ball hit squarely on my eye, and when my head snapped back, I heard, rather than felt, the explosion as I was knocked to the ground. I looked up through my right eye and saw my brother rushing toward me with a terrified look on his face. I couldn't open my left eye at all, and that whole side of my face was sticky and wet.

As Fritz helped me into the House, Rob, who hadn't moved, called after me, "Sorry, honeybunch. Bet that feels better though." I knew then, as if there had been any question, that he'd done it on purpose—he was too good a player for it to have been an accident. If it had been Fritz or David, I would have taken it in stride—it also wouldn't have hurt so much. But Robert was twenty-six years old. After that, whenever either of my uncles was around, I kept to myself.

My aunts Maryanne and Elizabeth usually spent those Saturday mornings and afternoons with my grandmother in the kitchen. Gam and Liz sat at a small chrome-and-tile table that jutted out from the wall next to the refrigerator like something you'd see in a 1950s-era diner, while Maryanne, in her tweed skirt, sweater, and low heels, leaned against the counter by a window that looked out onto the backyard—maybe to make sure Donald or Robert wasn't trying to break any of David's bones.

It would have been like me to try to insert myself into their conversation, like a kid jumping double Dutch looking for just the right opening, but their conversations never skipped a beat and there was no room for me. If they'd been in the library, with everybody sitting down, I wouldn't have minded listening in silence to their chatter. We could have gone out to lunch or gone shopping, but nobody ever suggested it. Standing in the middle of the kitchen felt awkward, so I left to find somewhere else to be.

It was during those long days in the House, with the boys playing games that excluded me and the women chatting in the kitchen about things that didn't concern me, that I started to turn inward. There were always people around, but we seemed never to make an impression on one another—or I didn't make an impression on them—so, instead, I wandered through the rooms of that big, empty house looking for somewhere to be alone.

Liz had not only the best bedroom, but the best room in the House—a spacious, sun-filled corner room, with a bay window overlooking the backyard. Given Liz's position in the family—the middle child, the younger girl, too young to have grown up close with Maryanne and Freddy and too old to relate to Donald and Robert—this always surprised me. I wondered if my grandfather had assigned the rooms on purpose, but then I realized the man simply didn't understand how space worked, given the bizarre asymmetry of the House, the design of which he oversaw and which he'd had built from scratch, and its lack of formal elegance. Once Fred had relegated Freddy, his heir apparent, to the Cell, he probably didn't care where his other kids slept. Liz had simply gotten lucky. Even though she had a full-time job at Chase Manhattan and her own apartment, a grim one-bedroom on the Upper East Side of Manhattan, with a western exposure blocked by a taller building across the street, she came to the House almost every weekend. She seemed to have no social life and maintained an unhealthy dependence on my grandparents until she got married, for the first time, in 1989, at the age of forty-seven. (Her dependence on Maryanne never waned. She even changed her will at Maryanne's instruction because, according to Maryanne, "If it weren't for me, Elizabeth would have left everything to a cat shelter or some bullshit." Liz had no children, so one can only imagine whom Maryanne might have recommended as a beneficiary.)

I loved hiding out in her room, and sometimes I dared to curl up on her bed. Usually, I sat on the floor and leaned against it or lay in a patch of sun by the window reading her magazines.

There were three transistor radios in the House—one in Dad's Cell, the second in Maryanne's bedroom, an uninviting square that looked like a room at an extended-stay business hotel, and the third in the kitchen, all always tuned to AM news or talk radio. Liz had a cassette player *and* cassettes—hers was the only room in the House with music.

When I was nine, she added Neil Diamond's *His 12 Greatest Hits* to her collection. I knew his music from the radio and the jukebox at Dante's, the Italian restaurant we went to with Dad a couple of times a month, but those were only a handful of singles. I'd never heard "Shilo" or "Brooklyn Roads" before, and I began to wish Liz wouldn't be at the House when I came by so I could listen to the tape, flipping the cassette back to the A-side when "Brooklyn Roads" ended, until it was time to leave. If she was around, I had to find somewhere else to go. Even if she was downstairs with Gam and Maryanne, I wouldn't have dared go to her room. It never occurred to me to ask if I could hang out in her room with her, just as it never occurred to her to invite me in, let me sit next to her on the floor sharing her popcorn, flipping through magazines, and listening to music.

I eventually stole the cassette from her. I knew it was wrong, but I wanted to be able to listen to it all the time. I could have asked my mother to buy it for me, or I could have used my allowance to buy it for myself, but neither of those things occurred to me, either.

My grandfather was rarely home on Saturdays, so even if Liz was camped out in her room, I still had options. When I was little, I sometimes sneaked into the foyer coat closet and shut the door behind me. My grandmother kept her fur coats there, and my grandfather's collection of hats, each carefully blocked within its own box, lined the shelves along three of the walls. The ceiling was at least twelve feet high, and after rolling around in the fur coats, I pulled out the stepladder and took down one of the hat boxes from the lower shelf, something I never would have done if my grandfather had been home. There was a mirror attached to the door that folded out so you could see yourself from three different angles. After I put the hat on my head and adjusted it so it didn't completely cover my face, I struck poses like a gangster.

Eventually I got tired of the smell of mothballs and the worry that I might get caught.

My grandparents' bedroom, a cool, large space two steps down from the upstairs hallway and directly above the living room, had the same floor plan and low-pile taupe carpeting. I tiptoed over the open floor between the door and the bed with trepidation, as if it were so many miles of enemy territory.

Gam's dressing room, an antechamber to the master bathroom, was far away from the door, but that was a destination worth taking risks to get to. There was a built-in vanity on either side where Gam kept her makeup and toiletries. Her perfumes, intricately carved bottles of cobalt and emerald and bordeaux, were arrayed in formation, the smallest in front. An enormous lead crystal bottle of Chanel No. 5 was set off to one side. I sat on the tufted ottoman and chose a bottle at random, brushing the stopper lightly against my wrists. The opposing walls were covered with mirrors that reached to the ceiling, reflecting off each other and creating an infinite sequence of images. There were so many of me, each copy diminishing in size as they re-ceded until I got lost trying to find the point just beyond per-ception, mesmerized by the way space seemed to unfold in the absence of space.

Sometimes I stayed there so long, I wonder if anybody thought to look for me or if they had even noticed I was missing.

The air in the House was inert, as if nobody had ever lived there at all, but I staked out these out-of-the-way spaces, no matter how dark or small, and imbued them with comfort and mys-tery. I could disappear into them, imagine them as wondrous, faraway empires.

As I grew older, being on my own at Gam's vanity, or in Liz's room, or in the basement where my grandfather's life-size Indian chief humidors loomed in the shadows, started to feel transgressive, as if I were breaking an unspoken rule and do-ing something indefinably wrong. The comfort began to bleed away and the mystery became tinged with dread, as if the rooms and closets and out-of-the-way corners were off limits and I was crossing a line nobody had actually drawn. Increasingly, an inchoate threat hovered over those safe spaces where I could be myself, spaces that got chipped away and chipped away until there was nowhere left, until I felt like I didn't even belong in my own skin. I couldn't define the potential consequences of being "caught" (just as I couldn't define what being caught even meant), I just knew that there would be consequences. I had somehow intuited what it was like to be my father growing up in that house. I was finally becoming conscious of something I'd known, at least on some level, all along—there was no way for me to fit into this family.

24

Dad inserted the key in the lock and then paused as if steeling himself before showing us his new apartment, a one-bedroom on the northwest corner on the top floor in Sunnyside Towers, yet another building my grandfather owned. When Dad had first brought us to the basement of the two-story walk-up a couple of years earlier, he'd been happy, as if a new adventure were starting. Now he was worn out, and the short walk down the dank hallway seemed to exhaust him.

There wasn't much furniture. A turntable sat next to the television, and he'd set up a ten-gallon tank with a couple of forlorn-looking goldfish. The fiberglass replica of the head and three-foot bill of the nine-hundred-pound swordfish he caught during a competition in Montauk in the early 1960s hung over the couch.

The apartment at least had a proper kitchen, a small room with clapboard cabinets and peeling linoleum and a refrigerator stocked with cans of Coke and Fresca, little bottles of clam juice, and two quarts of milk. Other than a bottle of Bosco chocolate syrup, there wasn't any food except for a couple of boxes of cereal and a five-pound bag of sugar in one of the cabinets. We usually ordered takeout, alternating between pizza and Chinese food.

Dad tried, but his judgment was always a little off. He took us to see *Serpico*, a movie about an undercover cop who gets shot in the face and in which a woman gets gang-raped, when I was nine. When we called my mother afterward to check in, she asked to speak to Dad after we told her what we'd been up to. As soon as he put the receiver to his ear, we could hear her screaming at him. He laughed it off, but I could tell it shook him. I don't think he was entirely sure what he'd done wrong.

We went to wrestling matches at Sunnyside Garden Arena—a square, smoke-filled auditorium with a boxing ring in the center, folding chairs arranged in rows on all four sides, and wooden bleachers along the walls. We saw Chief Jay Strongbow, André the Giant, and Bruno Sammartino, the most famous wrestler at the time, but the crowd was rowdy and beer-soaked, and we stopped going after somebody in the audience set off a smoke bomb and, in the ensuing chaos, folding chairs started flying through the air.

It was better when we spent quiet nights in the apartment watching TV shows like *All in the Family* and *Sanford and Son* as Dad got steadily drunk and then slipped off to his room before it became too noticeable.

The couch didn't pull out, so Fritz and I spread sheets and blankets on the floor and lay on top of them watching late-night episodes of *The Twilight Zone* or *Chiller Theatre*. The opening sequence of the latter—a bloodstained, six-fingered hand writhing up from a muddy swamp with a dead tree in the background—usually scared me more than the actual movie. But what kept me awake, listening to the hum of the fish tank's air filter, was wondering what the next day would be like.

Dad often claimed to have places to be while we were there. After he left the apartment, Fritz and I would wander around the neighborhood, stopping at the corner candy store to buy as much candy as we could afford or splurging on a Pinky ball. We played catch on the roof until one of us threw it too hard or wildly and it sailed over the edge.

In the months after my parents returned to Jamaica from Marblehead, Dad had become a volunteer ambulance driver for a firehouse in Hillcrest, a neighborhood a couple of miles north of the Highlander. When they were still together and Fritz and I were little, we went there every year for the Christmas party.

He still filled in occasionally for an evening shift. I think it was an excuse to see his friends from the old days, some of whom were still around, and he brought us with him to show us off, he said. We spent the evening sitting in the cab of a fire engine listening to talk radio or on the rear bumper of the ambulance watching him smoke until it became clear there was nothing for him to do and we went home.

A couple of weeks after we got back from camp the next summer, Fritz found a box of old 78s in the incinerator room down the hall from our apartment in Jamaica (we still burned garbage back then). The box was so heavy that neither of us could lift a corner of it off the floor, and we had to push it across the hallway carpet to our apartment.

When Dad came to pick us up, I could tell that he'd "been away." His clothes were neater and his hair perfectly slicked back—he looked brighter. When he saw the records on the floor by the front door, he gave a whoop. He dropped down on one knee and started flipping through them, calling out names of songs he knew with the excitement of a child.

We were going back with him to Sunnyside and he asked my mother if he could take the records. She said yes—which was generally the average length of their interactions back then—and when Dad bent to pick the box up, I looked at him skeptically. But he rolled up his sleeve and flexed his bicep. I squeezed it with both hands, and he lifted me up until both of my feet floated above the ground. He lifted the box as if it weighed nothing, hoisted it on his shoulder, and carried it all the way to the car.

When we got back to Sunnyside, we spent the entire day listening to song after song. The box contained everything from Benny Goodman to "Yes, We Have No Bananas" to Orson Bean's "I Ate the Baloney" and the truly bizarre "The Great Crepitation

Contest of 1946—The Battle at Thunderblow, Windesmear vs. Boomer."

The three of us ate pizza and drank Coke while we sat on the floor, the records spread around us while Dad rediscovered songs he hadn't heard since he was a kid. All of it was new to Fritz and me, but the best part was watching him have fun.

I'd never realized how much Dad liked music. He had two eight-track tapes in the car that we listened to in rotation: the studio version of *Jesus Christ Superstar*, with Murray Head instead of Ben Vereen singing the part of Judas, and the Who's recording of *Tommy*, which was released six years before—and was light-years better than—the movie version. He had a few albums in the apartment, but most of them were recordings of Scottish bagpipe music, which didn't bear repeated listening, or comedy routines from the Smothers Brothers and W. C. Fields.

One of the last records we pulled from the box was the Weavers' 1951 Decca recording of "Kisses Sweeter Than Wine," pressed in burgundy shellac. The line that initially stuck out when I first heard it was "Our children numbered just about four," which made me laugh because the couple singing the song didn't seem to know exactly how many kids they had. But there was something else about the song, too, that prompted me to ask Dad to play it for me again.

He looked at his watch—it was already time for *Sanford and Son*, and I was surprised when I looked out the window to see the sun starting to set. A couple of hours later, after Ralph Kramden threatened to send Alice to the moon for the last time, we were setting up our makeshift bed, and I asked Dad to put the song on again.

He didn't need to ask which one. He crossed the room to the turntable, put the album on, and set the needle down. The bridge—the plucked strings and then Ronnie Gilbert's voice arching over everything—filled me with longing. I never understood why things moved me the way they did, why, at the bottom of everything, there lurked an aching and a sense of irretrievable loss I couldn't consciously locate in my own life. *Their* lives in the song seemed so simple, something to aspire to, something anybody could achieve. Dad knew that was impossible. He also knew that I didn't yet.

When the needle began to scratch, he said, "One more time?"

"Yes, please," I answered. And he stood up, walked again through the dark to the turntable, and moved the needle back to the first groove. The initial scratch, and then the song began again. He sat back down and listened with me. I watched him from my sleeping bag, cigarette smoke curling around him, lit only by the light of the streetlamp coming through the window. It was the most still I'd ever seen him. He played the song for me over and over and over until I fell asleep.

For a while after that, things were OK.

Fritz had a softball game and Dad was running an errand, so I was left to my own devices. I was going to play handball against the side of the building, but we'd lost our last Pinky ball off the roof and I didn't have enough money to buy a new one. I started rooting around to see if I could find some jacks. I was going through Dad's closet when I found a shoebox. In bold letters, he'd written 2ND LT. FRED C. TRUMP, JR. Dad had been in the army?

I took the box into the living room and sat on the floor in front of the couch. When I opened it, there were some smaller, black boxes, an envelope marked FIRST OFFICE (SOC), and another marked PHOTOS, DO NOT BEND, as well as some loose medals tucked away to the side. I took these out first. Some of them looked just like the riflery medals I earned at camp. Some were strips of colored ribbons wrapped around small metal bars. I was about to arrange them on the coffee table when Dad came home.

He put the brown paper bag he was carrying on the floor and walked over. He was about to say something when he realized what I had and sat down heavily on the couch next to me.

If I'd known the word, I would have said he looked wistful. As I took out each medal and certificate and photographs of him in different uniforms and laid them on the table, he explained what they were for, why he'd received them, and the names of the men he posed with. He also told me about the planes he stood next to in some of the pictures. There was something else in him then—a diffidence, as if talking about his accomplishments or showing any pride in them was unseemly.

He rarely talked with me about flying, although I knew he and Fritz sometimes parked by the runways at JFK with a pair of binoculars to watch the planes take off. He told me that a lot of the terms we used in boating, like "upwind" and "downwind," "knots," and "rudders," were the same used in flying. Both sails and wings operate according to Bernoulli's principle. I don't think I was ever on a plane Dad flew—if I was, I was too young to remember—but I'd seen him pilot enough boats to recognize that transformation, the beautiful certainty that came with his extraordinary skill.

But flying had its own abstract international language, developed to communicate with the ground crew. When he was at the TWA training facility in Kansas City, he had had to commit to memory an ever-expanding list of abbreviations and acronyms that covered everything from weather (GNDFG for ground fog) to the most technical aspects of negotiating large airports. "DE-CIDE," a voice from the control tower commanded whenever a plane had descended low enough to land but still had an opportunity to pull up if necessary.

He loved what he called the clipped efficiency of it. It was one of the few things that made sense to him.

When I reached for one of the small black velvet boxes, slightly bigger and more rectangular than the others, he stopped me.

"That's enough for now. Fritz will be home soon. Let's put this stuff away."

He carefully placed everything back in the shoebox in the same order I'd found it.

The next time I was alone in the apartment, I went through it again. When I found what I was looking for, I opened it. Inside was a pair of gold wings with the letters TWA stamped in red in the center. I had no idea what they were for, and Dad never told me.

Dad had promised to take us fishing. I went to his bedroom to see if he was awake. He lay in his light blue boxers and white undershirt, the greying sheets twisted around his long, lanky frame. As I watched from the doorway—I rarely ventured beyond the threshold—I thought he was asleep, but then I saw that he'd already lit a cigarette. When he heard me, he pressed his thumb and forefinger against his eyelids, willing himself to sit up.

He squinted over at me through the smoke, which curled, blue and grey, toward the ceiling. "Can you get me a Coke?"

I walked backward two steps into the hallway and turned in to the kitchenette. Without turning on the overhead light— the fluorescent glare of which made the cramped space look even more depressing—I opened the refrigerator, grabbed a Coke, and walked tentatively to his bedside with my offering, then hopped back to the doorway. I waited while he popped the tab, threw it in the ashtray, and took a long swallow. He struggled to get his eyes back open. It was three thirty in the morning.

"You ready?"

"Ready."

"Is Fritz up?"

"Yeah."

"OK. Five minutes and we'll get going."

I don't know how he did it, but he struggled out of bed, got dressed, packed up some gear, got us into the car, and began the three-hour drive in the dark to Montauk.

It was a dull, grey day, and rain started falling as we drove east. For a change, he didn't turn on the radio, and we made the trip in silence. By the time we arrived, a cold, steady drizzle was falling. We stopped at a coffee shop to get some drinks and then pulled over next to a pay phone. Dad left the engine running while he went to make a call and the windshield wipers swiped futilely at the rain. Fritz turned on the radio. I poured a container of creamer into Dad's coffee. It curdled. I took a sip and burned my tongue.

After what seemed like a long time Dad finished the call, put the receiver back in its cradle, and slumped against the phone booth, bent like a question mark. By then he was almost emaciated and looked so depleted he could barely hold himself up. Finally, he straightened up and walked back to the car. When he slid into the driver's seat, his bony knees bumped against the steering wheel. Raindrops clung to his hair, which was plastered to his head. After shutting the door, he didn't say anything and didn't move for a very long time. Fritz and I waited, but we both knew the fishing trip had been canceled.

Dad switched off the radio and cleared his throat.

"We're not going to be able to use Jim's boat today." He

paused. I'd never heard of Jim. "His daughter was in a bad car accident last night. She's in the hospital. She . . ." He stopped again as if evaluating how much he could say. Fritz and I leaned closer. "She might not make it. A truck swerved into her lane and hit her car head-on." Then he added, "She went through the windshield."

I shifted back in my seat. I could see the road, black and slick with rain; the truck jackknifed; the car crumpled by the side of the road; shards of glass glistening in the chaotic light of the headlights. I could see her lying on the side of the road, inert.

I didn't believe a word of it. He had paused too much, given too much detail. I assumed Dad had either forgotten to charter a boat or, somewhere on the road during the long, wet drive, he realized he just didn't have it in him to spend the day with us on the open water under that leaden, grey sky.

When we got back to Sunnyside that night, Dad drank so much he passed out on the toilet. There was only one bathroom in the apartment, and by nine o'clock Fritz and I were desperate to use it. We tried to get in, but Dad's bony knees were pressing against the door, so we couldn't open it enough to squeeze through. I'm not sure what we would have done if we had. Part of me was glad—his khakis were rolled loosely around his ankles, and I could see all the way up the side of his pale leg. I couldn't see much more and wanted to keep it that way.

Fritz and I had no choice but to make our way down the hallway, knocking on the doors of neighbors we'd never spoken to. Finally, somebody opened theirs and we explained our bathroom was out of order; they let us in.

When we got back to the apartment, Dad was still unconscious. Without saying a word to me, Fritz picked up the phone and called Mom. When she answered, he said, "Come get us."

25

I loved my mother extravagantly, with the unconditional, un-requited love of a medieval knight. I had become exquisitely attuned to her moods and expert either at defusing them or empathizing with her. My job, perhaps the most important job in my life, was to comfort her, anticipate her needs, and make her feel like she was the center of the universe, to take the sting out of her belief that she'd been robbed.

When I had enough money, I bought her flowers on the way home from school, just in case she was sad. I let her sleep in on school days if she was depressed and took the bus or subway to Forest Hills so she didn't have to drive me. I bought her expensive gifts for her birthday and Christmas with the gift money I got from my grandparents—jewelry from Bloomingdale's or Lladró porcelain figurines. She developed a taste for Waterford crystal, and two or three times a year I added to her collection, a glass or two, or even a decanter, at a time.

I had just gotten home from school and was going to change out of my uniform when Mom called to me from her bedroom. I didn't get in trouble much, so I didn't think it was because of anything I'd done.

She was perched on the edge of her bed looking stricken, a slightly crumpled piece of loose-leaf paper pinched lightly between her thumb and index finger, as if she didn't want to be touching it at all. She held it out to me and, with her eyes downcast, said, "This came in the mail today."

On any other occasion, I would have climbed onto the bed to comfort her, either with a hug or simply sitting next to her silently, and I'd sit there until she moved—or I'd sit next to her forever if she didn't.

I took the note. To my relief, the writer appeared to be somebody my age, because it was written in a child's hand.

Dear Mrs. Trump,

I am writing about your daughter, Mary. You might think you know her but you don't. She pretends to be friendly, but she is <u>unkind</u> and duplicitous.

I stopped, confused. The language had matched the handwriting at first, but what did "duplicitous" mean?

Yes, she's "popular," but have you ever wondered why? Do you think it's because there's something special about her? Maybe it's because her grandfather, Mr. Trump (your father-in-law), is on the school's Board and that's why the teachers treat her with favoritism at the expense of the other children. It's a shame people feel they can't be honest because Mary is, quite simply, a mean girl and a hypocrite. If it weren't for your family connections, nobody would give her the time of day.

You're her mother, I'm sure you love her. But believe me, no one else does.

As I read, a weird numbness spread across my body, as if I weren't in the room anymore. When I finished, I came into my body again and began to shake. My eyes stung and the heat rose in my cheeks, a combination of despair and shame. When I handed the piece of paper back to my mother, tears were already running down my cheeks, but I wasn't crying yet. My arms hung limply at my side. I thought if I moved, I'd break in half. Mom didn't reach for me right away, perhaps waiting to see my reaction, but when she did, I collapsed in her arms, sobbing with a grief more extreme than anything I'd ever felt before.

Mom let me go and I fell in a heap at her feet, clutching her legs and still crying. She picked up the phone and called Mrs. Eaton, my fifth-grade teacher, whom I loved despite the fact that she insisted on teaching us how to diagram sentences. Mrs. Eaton recommended that I stay home the next day and she would discuss the matter with the headmaster to see if there was anything they could do. My mother asked if I wanted to speak to her, but I shook my head. I couldn't stop crying.

After she hung up, my mother brought me to my room and came back a few minutes later with cinnamon toast and tea as if I were home with a cold, but I had no appetite.

After I read my first-ever piece of hate mail, the divide that existed between me and other people became a chasm. The shift wasn't obvious or dramatic, but the letter accelerated the process of cutting me off from the rest of the world.

I wondered which of my classmates wrote the letter—and which of their parents had composed it. It could have been anyone in my grade; there were only twenty of us. Maybe it was even somebody I considered a close friend. Maybe there *were* people who thought that I got preferential treatment because of my grandfather. And maybe I did—but how could I explain all of the ways in which that either wasn't true or didn't matter?

I had friends—*I had friends*. My teachers liked me; I thought they respected me—didn't they? I tried hard—to be good, to be better. But how could I know? How could I ever be sure of anything?

But there was more going on. An agenda existed behind the composition of this letter, and it was the agenda of an adult.

How could I understand the dark, obscure motives of an adult? Was I so bad that my mother needed to have the terrible truth about me revealed to her?

I sat on my bed determined to figure out what I'd done—or what somebody believed I'd done.

It was getting harder for me to ignore the fissures that were opening up all around me, harder to keep my humiliation—about the knots in my hair or my father's few but almost always drunken appearances—at bay.

Reading that letter fundamentally changed who and how I was at school. The change wasn't immediate, probably not even noticeable.

I developed a wariness that affected my interactions with other people. More significantly, the letter underscored what I had already begun to intuit long before, the truth of who *I* was that would shadow me for the rest of my life. No matter what I accomplished, no matter how I lived or who I became, I would never be good enough.

The one question I never asked, that I never thought to ask over the course of that long, dark day, was, why did my mother show me that letter? Why had she wanted me to read it in the first place?

My mother kept a basket on the high shelf in the coat closet by the front door. Every once in a while she took it down and pulled out a folder or a manila envelope. Her movements seemed surreptitious to me, and I wondered what she was hiding. I was home alone one day and decided to find out. I dragged the stepladder from the laundry room and set it in front of the closet. I had tried before, but even on tiptoe I couldn't reach the basket. That day, I finally could, and I pulled it off the shelf.

I sifted through the bank statements, canceled checks, and

letters until I found an envelope labeled "birth certificates." I held my breath as I opened it. Perhaps this was the answer. I pulled out three official-looking documents, and one of them was, indeed, my birth certificate, filled out in black and white with my parents' names, my time and date of birth, and my footprints.

I felt a wild, unexpected disappointment. I'd never thought about it consciously, but I didn't want to be from these people. It would have been so much easier if I'd been found under a rock.

26

We barely got through the door when Dad told Fritz, "You've got homework to do." Without complaint or comment, Fritz took his book bag into the bedroom.

Until Fritz entered high school, we never quite knew what to expect when we spent the weekend with Dad. In the mornings, his mood could be dark, or he could be unexpectedly happy and energetic. In the evenings, there was no way to determine if his optimism was based on an alcohol-fueled fantasy of possibility or if he was genuinely happy to have us with him, just as there was no way to know if his inscrutable gloom was the result of a bad day or the result of his surveying the bleak landscape of his life. Whether the optimism survived the dawn or the sunrise shattered it into pieces was impossible to predict.

One thing we could count on was that, except on rare occasions, Dad wasn't mean, and I had never known him to be stern, so none of our previous experiences with him prepared us for his new role as disciplinarian. There was a new, grim sameness to our time with him. We stopped going places with him—no early-autumn Mets games or day trips to Montauk—and the quiet, meant to be conducive to studying, became stultifying. It was as if he suddenly realized he had to parent and overcorrected.

Dad began to focus on Fritz's report cards, littered every semester with Cs and Ds and teachers' comments about his bad attitude and worse work ethic. Fritz wasn't a natural student, but he'd always managed to get by. He was popular, good-looking, athletic, and funny; he was the favorite of even those teachers whose classes he blew off or did poorly in. But Fritz would be applying to college soon, and now his grades mattered; getting into a good school mattered.

I never kidded myself that I was as important as my brother. Usually, I was the third wheel, tagging along and keeping up. Dad and I had our moments of synchronicity, but they almost always happened when the two of us were alone.

The two and a half years Fritz had with Dad before I came along made him simultaneously more sensitive to and more forgiving of Dad's transgressions. But those early memories also made Fritz idolize Dad, which gave him expectations that our father could never meet. Eventually those illusions of Dad's greatness shattered when he started to show up to Fritz's soccer games to cheer loudly and drunkenly from the sidelines, or when he was too drunk to show up at all.

The shift in Dad's attitude toward my brother accompanied his slide into almost unremitting gloom. It was harder to tell the difference between his being drunk and his being sober. And his focusing so much on grades put enormous pressure on Fritz. Dad's solution made the situation worse. His plan wasn't to help him or to hire a tutor. Instead, he banished Fritz to the bedroom down the hall and left him there, where he sat for hours, textbooks and notebooks spread around him on the bed. Sometimes whole weekends went by with Fritz emerging only briefly to get something from the refrigerator or join us for increasingly awkward meals. Other than that, Fritz never made a sound. He started getting horrible stomachaches, but never complained.

While Fritz studied, if that's even what he was doing, Dad and I sat together on the couch watching TV. He drank vodka and chain-smoked his Marlboro Reds; I drank Coke and inhaled his secondhand smoke. The silence coming from the room down the hall was difficult to ignore. Out of solidarity with Fritz, I didn't talk to Dad or suggest we play games. Dad remained silent for his own reasons, maybe as a way to maintain an atmosphere of studious seriousness. Who knows. I don't think even he did.

After months of inhabiting this strange, dark world with Dad, Fritz hit his breaking point. One Friday in December, my mother took us into Manhattan to see the Christmas tree at Rockefeller Center and the holiday show at Radio City Music Hall. Afterward, she planned to drop us off at Dad's place in Sunnyside.

She was just about to take the left turn off Queens Boulevard when Fritz, sitting in the front passenger seat, said quietly, "I don't want to go."

Mom appeared not to hear him and made the turn.

Fritz said more loudly, "I'm not going. I can't." His breath caught on the last word.

Mom looked at me in the rearview mirror. She didn't say anything at first, just kept driving down the side street. We were only a few blocks away.

From the back seat, I saw Fritz tense up.

"OK," Mom said. "Mary, what do you want to do?"

"I don't care," I said.

She made a U-turn and we went home.

27

I came to like being in the hospital—at least after the worst of it was over. As I got older, they put me in the adult ward if there was a free bed. Sometimes, I even had the room to myself. It was cool and quiet, and—because of the drugs—I couldn't concentrate or think too deeply about anything. Some of the rooms had televisions, all of which seemed permanently tuned to PBS.

A pattern started to emerge: most of my attacks occurred in spring and autumn, fewer in winter. I never had one at camp, which made sense, or when I stayed with my father, which made none. I also tended to be admitted frequently over the holidays—Thanksgiving, Christmas, New Year's Eve, sometimes even my birthday. I came to like that, too.

But the stress on my body added up. It took me longer to bounce back after I'd been released. I went back to school right away, but I'd be exhausted for days. The medication made me jittery and anxious, and I had trouble falling asleep.

There was a Methodist church on the corner of Highland Avenue and 164th Street that I walked past on the way home if I took the subway to Parsons Boulevard. An adjacent parking lot had been cut into the side of the hill, and a retaining wall by the delivery entrance separated the lot from the church's front lawn. Starting when I was around eleven years old, instead of heading straight home, I sometimes slid through a hole in the chain-link fence and sat on the concrete ledge with my legs dangling over the edge.

I thought about jumping. Aside from dark circles under my eyes and a slight forward hunch of my shoulders, both of which disappeared a couple of days after being discharged, there was nothing to prove I'd suffered. I wanted to bleed or break. I longed for a scar or any recognizable sign that would force people to notice that something had happened to me, something that demanded a response.

The wall wasn't high enough to do any real damage. Even so, in the end, I couldn't make myself jump. I couldn't overcome my instinct for self-preservation. I didn't want to hurt myself, really; I just wanted to find out what it would be like if people knew, whether anything would change.

I had a follow-up visit with Dr. Goldman, my pulmonologist, a few days after I got home from my most recent visit to the hospital. I was still tapering off my steroids and, although I was already back in school, I still felt weak and a little shaky.

I sat on the exam table slightly hunched over because my upper back muscles were extremely tight, especially between my shoulder blades. The doctor's hands were cool. When he grabbed my shoulder and his thumb pressed against my back as he positioned the stethoscope, my muscles relaxed, making me feel faint with relief.

He listened for a few seconds, then asked me to take a few deep breaths. "Your lungs sound good," he said. "Any problems since you've been home?" I shook my head.

"OK. Get dressed and meet me and your mom in my office. I've got some good news for you."

Dr. Goldman was sitting behind his desk writing notes in my chart when I came in and sat next to my mother.

"I forgot to ask," he said, after he put his pen down. "How's your cat?"

"Cats," I said. "We got two kittens."

His eyes narrowed slightly.

My mother, her voice pitched a little higher than usual and sounding defensive, said, "She gets her allergy shots every week."

"Well, that's something." His voice sounded neutral, but I sensed a tension between them. He checked his notes. "Is the allergist still Dr. Stewart?" She nodded. "I'll want to follow up with him as well. Now, for the main reason you're here."

He opened his desk drawer and pulled out a cylinder, half metal, half plastic. "This," he explained, "is a rescue inhaler." He pulled the two halves apart, turned the plastic tube ninety degrees, and attached the other end to the metal half so the whole thing looked like a truncated L.

"Once you've reattached the top like this, give it a few good shakes. Exhale all the way and then put the tip of the plastic opening in your mouth—make sure you seal your lips around it—and then push the ends together, inhaling deeply at the same time, like this." He pantomimed the movement, and when he inhaled it looked like his eyes were bugging out of his head. "You might have to practice that part a bit. When you've inhaled all the way, hold your breath for a few seconds, and then breathe normally. That's it."

He squeezed the inhaler and a fine mist sprayed through the air. "This is medicine called Alupent. Take it as soon as you feel your chest getting tight."

"And that'll help?"

"Yep. It'll clear you right up."

"Really?"

"Really."

I didn't quite believe him. It didn't seem possible for the solution, after all this time, to be so simple. I'd learn later that the medication had been around for several years already, but it may have been considered inappropriate to give to a younger child due to risk of overdose.

"Before you go, remember—take it when you need it, follow the directions, keep it clean. And don't sleep with the cats. The nurse will have it all written down for you before you leave. Now go sit in the waiting room. I need to talk to your mom for a couple of minutes."

I left the room but didn't close the door all the way. Instead of heading to the waiting room as I'd been told, I stood very quietly in the hallway.

I heard Dr. Goldman clear his throat. "Mrs. Trump, I obviously haven't been able to convince you to get rid of the cats, but I cannot stress how important it is that you bring Mary to the hospital at the first sign of trouble, day or night—no matter what time it is. The inhaler will help, but it won't always work. Again, at the first sign of trouble, you must bring her in. You *cannot* wait."

I had never heard anybody speak to my mother like that. If my mother responded, I didn't hear it.

"Do you have any questions?" Dr. Goldman finally asked.

Again, nothing.

"Then I'm sure I'll be seeing you both soon."

I ran to the waiting room before my mother reached the door.

When we got into the car, Mom seemed annoyed, like a child who'd been chastised. I rested my hand on her forearm. "Mom, I really don't want to get rid of the cats."

"I know," she said.

I had stopped rushing to my mother's room as soon as an attack started. I waited in my room until waiting was no longer an option, because waiting allowed me to postpone the torment of the moment when my mother, ignoring all of the evidence in front of her, said in her tired, apathetic way, for the twentieth or thirtieth time, "OK, get in."

Having an inhaler would change everything.

The first time I used it, the mist spread through my lungs, dilating my bronchial tubes and opening up my airways. The relief was almost instantaneous and so profound, I cried. I hadn't allowed myself to believe it could be true. It was like a pocket miracle. Now if I had trouble breathing in the middle of the night, I could stay in my room until morning, sparing myself the added agony of hearing my mother's normal, steady breathing as I waited for rescue.

I felt invincible. I didn't have to go to the hospital. When I told my mother the next morning, she smiled. She probably felt freed from the burden I'd placed on her.

Then, one morning after an attack, I was still struggling to breathe. Mom, secure in the knowledge that I had the inhaler, asked if I wanted to stay home. I waited for her to offer another option, but she didn't, and I knew better than to ask. She left me at home in my bed with a cold-air humidifier, cinnamon toast, and a cup of tea.

The doctor had said to follow the instructions—he had failed to mention what would happen if I didn't.

Not long after my mother left for the day, I was hanging over the humidifier, my weight on my forearms. My mouth had to be right next to the opening where the cold vapor came out in order for it to do any good. This exhausted me and increased the tension in my back. When I pulled away to give my muscles a break, my face, hair, and pajama top were soaking wet.

I took my inhaler again. I sat up against my pillows, which I stacked against the wall, and kept my breathing as slow and even as I could in order to postpone as long as possible my need for another dose of Alupent.

The air conditioners in our apartment had been installed improperly, and whenever we used them, condensation softened the drywall around them, causing it to bubble. I was too tired to read, so I passed the time poking my fingers through the air bubbles.

I was supposed to wait four hours between doses, but inevitably I couldn't. I became dependent on the clock, needing to know how many minutes had passed since my last dose, trying to gauge how many more minutes I could possibly last before I reached for my inhaler again. Four hours, then three hours, then two hours, then one. When I was reduced to watching the minutes, I knew I was past help.

Finally, when I rolled over and took a hit from my inhaler, nothing happened.

Nothing.

Weeks later, I hurt my left wrist playing softball. The school nurse thought it might be broken, so when my mother picked me up from school, she suggested my mother take me to the emergency room.

I'd never been there in the middle of the day before. Whenever I came in with an asthma attack, I was rushed in immediately, with urgency. This was the first time I'd been left in the waiting room. After an hour, I wondered what was taking so long.

My mother had gone upstairs to the Women's Auxiliary offices to catch up on paperwork, leaving me with instructions to have the nurse call her when the doctor was able to see me. Every seat was full, with patients and relatives of patients, and there was no room to walk around. I didn't want to go outside and risk missing my turn, so after three hours of waiting, I wandered over to the nurses' station. The two women working behind it were both busy, but one recognized me from my previous visits, even though it was probably the first time she'd ever seen me standing upright.

"What brings you here?" she asked, barely looking up from her paperwork.

I raised my arm so she could see the Ace bandage wrapped around my wrist and hand.

"That's a nice change of pace." She went back to her work, but when I didn't move, she said, "Where's your mom?"

"She went up to the office. I was just wondering about the wait. It's been a few hours."

She slid her chair back, threw some file folders into a box on top of a filing cabinet, and rolled back to her desk. "A car drove through a red light and crashed into a bus full of elementary school kids. It's chaos." She shook her head. Every time the swinging doors to the ER opened, I heard the screams.

"That's awful."

I had turned back to find a seat when she said, "That's not the reason for your wait, though." I turned back and she jabbed her pen at my wrist. "Broken bones aren't life threatening."

When I was very little, I had loved being read to, but when I started sounding out the words to *The Cat in the Hat* with our neighbor Meghan, a world that had never existed sprung up before me fully formed. Reading, I realized, was a superpower.

My parents never put limits on the books I read or the number of books I could buy, so at every Scholastic Book Fair, I ordered whatever appealed to me. I read series like Frog and Toad and stand-alone picture books like Maurice Sendak's *Where the Wild Things Are*, but no story resonated with me like *Sylvester and the Magic Pebble*, by William Steig.

It's not the book Steig is most known for, but it quickly became my favorite. It was the first book I asked my mother to read to me when I was sick or too tired to read on my own.

Sylvester is a young donkey who lives with his parents, Mr. and Mrs. Duncan. The three of them are a very happy little family. One rainy spring day, Sylvester, who collects interesting pebbles, goes to a nearby lake to search for new ones to add to his collection. Along the way, he finds a perfectly round, bright red pebble. He picks it up and as he's holding it in his hoof, he begins to feel cold. He wishes the rain would stop.

And it does.

When he wishes the rain to begin again, dark clouds gather and raindrops fall to the ground. When he wishes for the sun to come out, the clouds disappear and the blue sky returns. Sylvester realizes that the pebble he's found must be magic. He decides to return home to show his parents, but as he crosses a sun-dappled meadow near Strawberry Hill, he crosses paths with a hungry-looking lion.

Lions, as Sylvester knows, prey on donkeys, and he becomes so terrified he panics. He says to himself, "I wish I were a rock." And he immediately transforms into a rock.

The lion strolls cautiously over to where his potential lunch had been a moment earlier. He sniffs the rock, he sniffs the ground around the rock, but to no avail. Mystified, the lion slinks off.

Although Sylvester is now safe from the lion, the magic pebble has fallen to the ground a few inches away from him. The magic, unfortunately, only works if the pebble is in contact with whoever is making the wish. Sylvester is stuck where he is.

When Sylvester doesn't return home, his parents become worried. They search everywhere but can find no sign of him.

Mr. and Mrs. Duncan fear the worst—that their little boy is gone forever—and they fall into despair.

As for Sylvester, he castigates himself for giving in to his fear. He could have wished the lion was a butterfly, he could have wished himself safely home. Instead, he became a rock. "Being helpless, he felt hopeless."

Seasons pass. The summer sun beats down on Sylvester the rock; autumn leaves fall in colorful piles around him; snow blankets him and he sleeps more and wakes less. Spring comes around again, flowers and trees bloom, but Sylvester remains in a deep slumber.

Sylvester's parents, although still devastated by the loss of their son, decide to go to the meadow for a picnic. They find a long, solid-looking rock and spread their picnic blanket over it. Sylvester hears his parents' muffled voices and slowly begins to awaken.

As Mrs. Duncan lays out the picnic, Mr. Duncan spots the

bright red pebble on the ground. "What a fantastic pebble. Sylvester would have loved it for his collection." With that, he places the magic pebble on the rock, and when Sylvester thinks, "I wish I were myself again, I wish I were my real self again!" he transforms back into Sylvester the donkey. The picnic goes flying. When his parents realize what's happened, everybody is delirious with happiness.

When they get home, the Duncans place the magic pebble in the safe because they already have everything they need.

I've heard this story referred to as "nightmare fuel," but as a child it soothed me. I found it a deeply comforting idea that in times of great stress or danger one could be protected in one's stillness and then become oneself again at the moment of wishing, that being still was the thing that protected me, and that, while I waited, someone might be looking for me, too.

As I got older, I often stopped by the candy store on the corner at 169th Street and Hillside Avenue and browsed through the books. Out of curiosity, I started picking up the monthly and quarterly science fiction digests squeezed into the slots of the rotating metal racks toward the back of the store. I'd never read science fiction before, but the cover art intrigued me, and soon I was reading stories by Isaac Asimov, Robert Heinlein, and Philip José Farmer.

After reading *David Starr, Space Ranger*, I tried to get my hands on everything Asimov had written since his first novel was published in 1950. (Reading it all would have been close to impossible, because he was incredibly prolific.) Besides the books I was required to read for school, I read nothing but science fiction, which took me away from everything that haunted me in real life—my asthma, my mother's depression, my father's drinking—in a way I'd never imagined was possible.

I was twelve when, out of idle curiosity, I took *In Cold Blood* down from the thinly populated bookshelf in our own living room. It had belonged to Dad, along with a copy of Kahlil Gibran's *The Prophet* and a thick tome by Gore Vidal. The dust jacket of Capote's book was long gone, so I had no way to know what it was about. I read it anyway.

"The village of Holcomb stands on the high wheat plains of western Kansas," it begins, "a lonesome area that other Kansans call 'out there.'" I was hooked by the end of the first paragraph. I'd never read anything like it. The prose—concise, precise— drew me in and pulled me along, but even setting the story aside, I also found it cold and ungenerous. A lot of the subtext went completely over my head, but it scared the hell out of me. *In Cold Blood* is the only book I ever read that kept me up all night in sheer terror.

Around the same time, I discovered an old paperback of Aleksandr Solzhenitsyn's *One Day in the Life of Ivan Deniso-vich.* One rainy day, when I was home alone, I set up my own little gulag in the living room. I sat on the floor with a bowl of very thin oatmeal, an old blanket wrapped around my shoulders, imagining what it must have been like for Ivan Denisovich Shukhov, falsely accused of being a spy for the Germans during World War II, as he froze and starved in the Soviet gulag.

The book that had the most impact on me was *The Martian Chronicles*, by Ray Bradbury. I'd already read several of his short stories and one or two of his novels, but I preferred the harder-edged science fiction of Asimov. But *The Martian Chronicles* transcended anything I'd read before. In it, Bradbury depicted a world I wanted to live inside, that I wanted to explore. While it could be terrifying and cruel, it could also be stunningly beau-tiful and weird and imaginative and poetic.

Almost every story I read seemed to cast a force field around me, within which I could carry these carefully wrought little worlds, but that also protected me against the real one. What I didn't realize at the time was that the force field, undetectably at first, also created a distance between me and everyone else.

I wanted to create my own worlds, too, so I began to sketch an idea for a short story. In it, two friends, a boy and a girl, discover an odd-looking book with a metallic cover, half-buried in a deserted lot. It turns out to be a journal written in English, but some of the symbols are foreign and some of the words unfamiliar. In the end, they learn that the journal is a warning from a future that is both dangerous and terrifying: it has been sent back in time by its writer in hopes that whoever finds it will change the course of history.

I labored over this story for weeks, especially the language of the journal. When I finished, I looked in the back of one of my favorite science fiction digests to find out how to submit it. I wrote the address on a manila envelope and brought it to the post office on the way home from school one day.

I waited every day for a response, alternately excited by the prospect it might be accepted and horrified by my hubris in sending it in the first place. Weeks passed. I'd almost forgotten about it when I got home from school one afternoon and found an envelope waiting for me on my pillow.

I felt a thrill of excitement, tinged with a bit of dread. I jumped onto my bed and opened the envelope carefully. The letter was typed, filling most of one sheet of paper, and signed in blue ink. The editor opened with his thanks for the submission and his regrets that they would not be able to publish my story.

He could have left it at that, and I would still have been grateful that he'd bothered, but he went on. He explained some of the story's deficiencies—the language, some of the weaknesses in the plot—but beyond that, he was very encouraging. He praised my imagination and creativity, as well as my courage in submitting the story in the first place.

"Again," he wrote, "while we cannot publish this work, please keep writing."

The editor must have intuited how young I was and understood the potential impact his response might have. It was so kind and generous and encouraging that I don't think I would have been much happier if my story had been accepted.

It was the kind of letter that deserved to be framed. Instead, I hid it between the mattress and box spring. I couldn't have said why, but I didn't want my mother to see it or even know about it. A few days later, I went to take the letter out—I wanted to read it again and bring it to school to show a couple of my friends—but it was gone.

I stripped my bed, felt inside the pillowcases, looked to see if it had fallen on the carpet underneath the bed. Maybe I had misremembered where I'd put it in the first place, so I went through all of my drawers and checked to see if I had placed it inside one of my books.

I never found the letter. I assumed my mother had, when she was changing my sheets, and thrown it away. But she never mentioned it, and I didn't dare ask, for fear of what she might say.

29

My mother came home and told me she had just run into Mrs. Lombardi, who had invited us for lunch. I hadn't been to the Lombardi house in three or four years.

When we arrived, the door to the room where they kept the board games was closed and lunch had already been set up in the dining room. The house hadn't changed, still washed in a greyish-green light, the furniture dark and heavy; it was unsettling to be back. Teresa and her older sister Maria joined us.

Mrs. Lombardi and my mother did most of the talking— gossiping about the neighborhood and catching up on what was going on with the other Lombardi kids. Angela, still living in the attic, was working in the city now; Luca had been transferred to a firehouse in Brooklyn and he hated the commute; Antonio had just gotten engaged.

I didn't say a word. I kept my eyes down.

After we finished eating, Mrs. Lombardi suggested we go to the living room and play keno. She'd started taking the bus down to Atlantic City with friends every other weekend and had become an avid gambler—penny keno and nickel slots. It was hard for me to picture her standing in front of a slot machine holding a plastic cup full of nickels, but I was happy for the diversion from the memories drifting through my head.

After Mrs. Lombardi explained the game, she gave each of us a certain number of pennies and we started to play. I lost the first few rounds, still figuring out how the rules worked, what the strategies might be.

The adults were still chatting and drinking coffee, but most of Mrs. Lombardi's attention was on the game. She won more rounds than anybody else, and she was gleeful about it. I lost every round we played.

I liked to win, but I'd always been a good sport. Even when I lost at things I cared about, I rarely got upset. I lost at Monopoly, badly, on an almost weekly basis, which had become a running joke among my friends.

As the afternoon progressed, and my store of pennies was almost depleted, I started to get angry. I couldn't hide it. When Maria joked about how seriously I was taking the game, I felt exposed and self-conscious. I felt them all looking at me, judging me and thinking that I was a spoiled brat who didn't know how to behave.

My mother looked on as if she were just a spectator.

Mrs. Lombardi won another round, but before she could claim her winnings, I picked up the bowl full of pennies from the center of the board and carried it to the other end of the room. I tried to make a joke of it, but I felt the weight of this terrible thing that had happened, of an injustice I couldn't understand or articulate. I wasn't giving those pennies back.

I didn't hang out with my old friends in Jamaica anymore. The route I took to the subway was along Hillside Avenue, so I rarely even ran into them. Even when we were close, my friends and I had never gone down the hill. I'd only ventured to South Jamaica when my father took us to the movies or my mother brought me to dance class.

The differences between the two communities on either side of Hillside had already been ingrained in me. As much as I loved the candy store and the Jamaican beef patty place that I stopped in almost every day on my way home, the tartan kilt, blazer, knee socks, and loafers I wore made it hard for me to blend in. But I never felt unsafe. On the white side of the neighborhood at the top of the hill, I had once felt comfortable, but I was never safe.

The worse home got, the more I missed camp, the more *necessary* became the respite that summers granted me. As soon as school was over, I wished the time away. During the lengthening days I sat on the bright yellow beanbag chair in my room, air conditioner blasting, a glass of ice and a pitcher of Lipton iced tea at my side, and read, or packed, or wrote bad poetry. I was still under the sway of *The Martian Chronicles*, and my days were suffused with the golden light that gleamed off the molten sands of the Martian desert. At night, when I looked out my window at the rising moon, I dreamed of Bradbury's "black velocities."

For a long time, I had taken my asthma, Dad's drinking, my mother's depression, my inability to relate to anybody in my family, even the knots in my hair, in stride.

But the more I recognized myself as a separate entity in the world whose appearance and actions were perceived to belong solely to me—separate and apart from my parents—the harder it became to ignore how other people looked at me and what they thought of me. I was tired. I wanted to be back where somebody always made sure my hair was brushed, where I knew what people thought of me. I wanted to be able to breathe.

At the beginning of every summer, Peter Greene, the head of drama, announced the end-of-summer musical. Even though drama was outside the usual scope of my interests, I loved being part of the show, and I auditioned every summer.

We were doing *Finian's Rainbow* (in order to make it work, Peter substituted "rich" and "poor" for "white" and "Black"). I got a small part singing "Necessity" with two other girls, and joined the crew as well.

I was there for almost all the rehearsals, either gathered around the piano with the rest of the cast or backstage working on the sets. Kim, an art major from the junior counselor training program, was in charge of designing the sets and helping us construct them. The rest of the crew and I spent a lot of time with her. I thought she was nice, but she was also sixteen and in charge—I was twelve and only there to do what I was told.

At one rehearsal, the two leads were at the piano working on "Something Sort of Grandish." Those of us who'd been working backstage took a break from painting and sat on some nearby benches to watch them. Kim sat a few seats away from me in a patch of sunlight. For the first time, I noticed the way the sun accentuated the highlights in her light brown hair. I noticed how beautiful her dark brown eyes were. I watched as she sang quietly along to the song.

After that, I looked out for her in the dining room. I looked forward to seeing her. Being around her made me feel happy and at ease.

I'd never had a crush before. I'd had boyfriends, but they never meant much. I had a boyfriend that summer. We spent time together at camp dances and he walked me back to my cabin at the end of the day. When we thought nobody was watching, we held hands. But it was Kim I thought about.

One morning, I got startled awake, out of breath, my heart pounding from a terrifying nightmare. It was still early, the cabin dark, everybody around me sleeping deeply. I tried to calm myself down, but when I played back the dream, my heart starting racing again.

Kim and I were in bed together, under the sheets, both of

us unclothed. As she slept, I gazed straight ahead as if looking into a camera, propped up on my elbow, my cheek resting on my hand. I had a relaxed smile on my face. I looked happy and confident.

I had never thought about kissing anybody before, let alone being naked in bed with them. I'd never thought about girls before at all. I talked about boys, because that's what girls were supposed to do, but I didn't think about them, either.

When my bunkmates started waking up around me, I pretended to be asleep. I worried that somebody could tell just by looking at me what I'd dreamed.

I got through the rest of the summer by avoiding Kim, spending less time working on the sets and more time with the cast.

The end of camp was as hard as always; my friends and I felt like—and acted like—the world was ending on the last day. But for the first time, I felt some relief mixed in with the sadness.

When I got home, though, I couldn't stop thinking about my feelings. It wasn't even about Kim. I had new information about myself that could potentially upend my life, but I didn't understand why. It felt wrong. *I* felt wrong.

When I walked into the locker room on the first day of school, I knew that I didn't belong there. Every day that passed, those feelings of wrongness intensified. I'd always been a tomboy, but I never wanted to be a boy, ever. The only way I could make sense of my feelings for Kim was that I was in the wrong body. Everybody in my world was straight, and I had no other frame of reference.

I couldn't talk to anybody, especially not my friends. I didn't have the words to describe what I was experiencing, and I felt such deep shame. If I didn't do something, though, the shame was going to swallow me whole. I began to worry that I was going to lose my mind if I held on to this secret.

Finally, I gathered every ounce of courage I had and told my mother I needed to talk to her. She was in her room, lying on her bed and propped up against her pillows, even though it was only midafternoon. I stood in front of her, rigid with fear.

She waited.

Before I could turn around and leave the room, I told her that I was worried that there was something wrong with me—that *I* was wrong. "I'm so wrong," I repeated, until my voice broke. I could barely speak but I still hadn't said the hardest part. "I don't think I'm supposed to be a girl." There was so much confusion and despair behind those words, I thought my heart would break with the pain of it.

My mother considered me for a minute, then said, "Do you think it would help if you talked to somebody?" It seemed she recognized that she wasn't equipped to help me, but she was willing to find somebody who could.

I dropped to my knees, because, somehow, she had managed to say the one right thing. I put my head on her lap, and I sobbed with relief until I thought I might fall asleep.

I waited for a few days for my mother to tell me she'd made an appointment with a therapist, but she never did. It didn't take long for me to realize she never would. I was left to live with it by myself.

Camp had always been a refuge; the good of camp was the fuel that helped get me through the ten long months at home. My feelings for Kim obliterated all that.

I didn't know anymore where I fit in. And I didn't know *how* to be.

PART III

The Serial Killer

Never to be found
What is like you now

Who were haunted all your life by the best of you
Hiding in your death

— W.S. MERWIN, "The Plaster"

32

1978

We were just getting ready to leave the apartment—two of my mother's friends from high school were visiting from out of town, and my mother had promised them a day in the city—when the phone rang.

"Fred needs to be transferred to Columbia-Presbyterian," my grandfather told my mother. He was the only person who refused to call my father Freddy. "Can you take him?" The question, as they both knew, was rhetorical. "George will be downstairs in ten minutes."

My mother felt put-upon, but as annoyed as she was, it didn't occur to her either to say no or to ask her friends if they minded taking the detour. We put our coats on and went downstairs to wait for my grandfather's limo.

Dad had returned to New York only a few days earlier. He'd been living in West Palm Beach for two years, an attempt to jump-start his life by putting some distance between him and his father. The experiment had ended when he was admitted to a Miami hospital with what the doctors eventually determined was an enlarged heart. He'd been so ill that my grandfather dispatched Maryanne, by now a prosecutor in the US Attorney's office, to bring him back to New York, and she dropped everything to do her father's bidding, just as my mother was doing now.

When Maryanne had arrived in Miami the previous week, Dad still had a nasogastric tube in place. He'd lost so much weight—he was down to less than 140 pounds—she almost didn't recognize her brother at first.

She stayed at a nearby hotel until he was stable enough to travel, at which point she accompanied him on the flight north. As soon as the plane landed at JFK, she took him to the House.

When my mother and I visited him that night, he had moved back into the Cell—the small, barren bedroom in which he'd grown up. It had only been two or three months since I'd seen him in Florida, but the transformation was shocking. He was gaunt and looked not just careworn but old, although he was only thirty-nine. Even at thirteen years old, I wondered why he hadn't been taken straight to the hospital.

That wouldn't happen until the next day, when Dad went to Jamaica Hospital. After a workup, the doctors there determined that his enlarged heart was the result of a diseased mitral valve, which was damaged beyond repair. My grandfather, who was on the hospital's board, had donated so much money that two years earlier the hospital had dedicated the Trump Pavilion for Nursing and Rehabilitation in honor of my grandmother.* Every courtesy was extended to him and members of his family, and the chief of cardiology called my grandfather personally to let him know that my father would need a valve transplant. At the time, replacing a human mitral valve with one from a pig was an experimental procedure, and the best place for that surgery was Columbia-Presbyterian Hospital, on the Upper, Upper West Side of Manhattan, he said. "We'll make arrangements for your son to be transferred to the new facility."

"I'll take care of it," my grandfather said. Then he called my mother.

---

* The name would be removed in March 2021, shortly after Donald's impeachment for inciting violence at the Capitol on January 6, 2021.

"Like Freddy, his future son-in-law, he wanted to be a pilot. Mike started taking flying lessons right out of high school, but the Depression—and his father, Willis Clapp—had put a stop to his dreams."

Gerald "Mike" Clapp, maternal grandfather

Courtesy of Mary L. Trump.

"Mike and Mary were an affectionate couple, and Mike clearly loved her, but he controlled pretty much everything and she had little or no say in any family decisions. As soon as Mary got sick, though, she became the entire focus of her husband's life, to the detriment of his relationships with his daughters."

Mary Rolfe Clapp and Mike Clapp

Courtesy of Mary L. Trump.

"Back in Kalamazoo, Linda had had friends, a community, and an environment that compensated her for what she wasn't getting from her parents."

Linda and Carol Clapp

Courtesy of Mary L. Trump.

"Mike sold his truck and used the proceeds to buy the restaurant— more of a clam shack, really— next door to the hotel. He knew nothing about the restaurant business, but it had once been a popular takeout place and the location was good, so he thought that, with the help of his wife and children, he could make it work."

Mike, Carol (seated), Mary, and Linda (seated) Clapp

Courtesy of Mary L. Trump.

Donald, Freddy, Elizabeth, Maryanne, and Robert (c. 1952)

Courtesy of Mary L. Trump.

"Linda joined the synchronized swimming team her sophomore year. Over the next three years the camaraderie with her teammates made life in high school manageable. The team performed all over South Florida and competed in statewide competitions."

Linda Clapp, far left

Courtesy of Mary L. Trump.

"My father's first cousin, Malcolm told me about the time Dad had flown him out to Montauk on a seaplane and how they'd anchored the plane next to the beach at Gurney's and ate steamers and lobster on the deck."

Freddy Trump

Courtesy of Mary L. Trump.

"In August 1958, Freddy Trump rented a plane from an airfield in Bethlehem, Pennsylvania, and flew with his best friend, Billy Drake, down to Nassau in the Bahamas for a short getaway before the fall semester at Lehigh University started."

Freddy Trump and Billy Drake

Courtesy of Mary L. Trump.

"At nineteen, Linda had never met anyone like Freddy Trump. Dressed in black slacks, white shirt, skinny black tie, and madras jacket, he was, at twenty, different from every boy she had ever known."

Courtesy of Mary L. Trump.

"When Linda turned twenty-one, she was accepted into the September class at National Airlines, a much bigger company that had routes all over the country. The new stewardesses were given a choice of three cities to be based in: Miami, Jacksonville, or New York. Linda picked New York."

Linda Clapp, front row, second from left

Courtesy of Mary L. Trump.

"Freddy's parents weren't pleased with the decision [to hold the wedding in Fort Lauderdale], but they didn't offer to help financially, either, and threw a New York reception when the newlyweds returned from their honeymoon."

Linda and
Freddy Trump (1962)

Courtesy of
Mary L. Trump.

"A ridiculously attractive couple, Freddy and Linda spent evenings in the city with his friends from Sigma Alpha Mu, the fraternity he belonged to at Lehigh, and the National Guard, going to restaurants and shows at the Copacabana on East Sixtieth Street."

Freddy and
Linda Trump

Courtesy of
Mary L. Trump.

"Whenever he took off from Idlewild, he flew over the Rockaway, Queens, beach house of his fraternity brother Stu and tipped his wings."

Cockpit of Freddy's Piper Cherokee

Courtesy of Mary L. Trump.

Freddy, Linda, and Frederick Crist Trump, III (1962)

Courtesy of Mary L. Trump.

Freddy with Fritz, his
first child (1963)

Courtesy of
Mary L. Trump.

"To get out from under his father's stifling control and blanket disapproval, Freddy applied to TWA, one of the largest airlines in the world and, under the ownership of Howard Hughes, the most glamorous. He was accepted into the first pilot class of 1964. In January, he moved halfway across the country to TWA's five-thousand-acre pilot-training facility a few miles north of Kansas City, Missouri, for four months to train on the Boeing 707, which, already embraced by TWA's greatest rival, Pan Am, was transforming air travel."

Freddy and Linda's apartment in Kansas City (1964)

Courtesy of Mary L. Trump.

"Freddy and Linda spent evenings in Kansas City sitting on the couch in their small living room, Fritz nearby in his crib, while she quizzed him using flash cards on which she'd written the technical terms he needed to commit to memory."

Freddy and Linda with
Two-no (1964)

Courtesy of Mary L. Trump.

"Freddy did so well in the program that when he graduated, TWA assigned him to fly the Logan Airport–LAX route. He, Linda, and Fritz moved to Marblehead, a small harbor town not far from Boston."

Freddy, Fritz, and Linda (1964)

Courtesy of Mary L. Trump.

Billy Drake and Freddy at a backyard barbecue, Marblehead (1964)

Courtesy of Mary L. Trump.

Linda, Annamaria Drake, and Freddy at a backyard barbecue, Marblehead (1964)

Courtesy of Mary L. Trump.

"My father's parents had never approved of Linda. They assumed from the start that she was a gold digger who glommed on to the first rich man she met. Given my grandmother's own upbringing as the tenth child of a crofter on a tiny island forty miles off the west coast of Scotland who worked as a domestic servant when she first arrived in New York, the double standard was a bit much."

Mary MacLeod Trump

Courtesy of Mary L. Trump.

"When I was younger, Dad borrowed boats from his friends—the serious kind of fishing boats that he had once owned—and drove us miles offshore chasing schools of striped bass or bluefish while he tried to hook something bigger and, for him, more challenging."

Freddy

Courtesy of Mary L. Trump.

"Nobody ever opened the door at the far end of the library, but there was a small covered porch that, despite the wrought-iron furniture that still sat out there, nobody used—it was just dead leaves and tumbleweeds and eerie silence. This porch was on the side of the House that always felt like no-man's-land, with a wide bed of ivy along the neighbor's property line and a grass path that led from the backyard to a small gate opening onto the front yard. There was something vaguely creepy about it."

From left to right: Linda Clapp Trump, Fred Trump Sr. (standing), Elizabeth Trump (my aunt), Elizabeth Trump (Fred's mother, seated)

Courtesy of Mary L. Trump.

"Dad traded the Piper Cherokee for a Cessna and bought a Chrisovich, a thirty-foot boat with a tuna tower, which he could drive much farther offshore for the kind of deep-sea fishing—for tuna and swordfish—he preferred. He often skirted the United States' sovereign maritime zone, twelve miles out, where he and Linda and whatever friends were with them saw sea turtles and whales. Once a humpback breached so close to them that Freddy, usually unflappable, gunned the engine because, as he later told Linda, he was terrified the whale might capsize the boat."

Freddy

Courtesy of Mary L. Trump.

"The man next to Dad was holding some papers right in front of the tiger's face. Dad was clearly calculating how to sign them without having to get his hand too close to the tiger's wide-open mouth. There's a self-consciousness in that calculation, as if he's aware he's supposed to look cool and unfazed but can't quite pull it off. His lips are drawn in a tight line and his entire body is tense. He can't help but look afraid. It's the only picture I've ever seen in which he looks like me."

Courtesy of Mary L. Trump.

"I became obsessed with that picture. When I was alone in my room, I spent too much time looking at it, as if it contained some secret I could unlock if only I looked hard enough. Sometimes at night when I couldn't sleep, I brought the picture to bed and studied it by the light of the streetlamp that streamed through the window.

The picture haunted me. Nothing about it seemed real except the way my father smiled at me."

Courtesy of Mary L. Trump.

Me, Montauk (1966)

Courtesy of Mary L. Trump.

"At camp, I discovered that I was an athlete, and I was good at almost every sport I tried, most of which, like archery and sailing, I'd never encountered before. I arrived at camp a proficient swimmer, but we swam in the bay every day, unless there was lightning, and I became an incredibly strong one. This opened up an entirely new world to me not just of skill and achievement, but of competition. I wanted to be better than other people, but more than anything, I just wanted to be better."

Courtesy of Mary L. Trump.

"The three of us spent a lot of time on the boat together, but on quiet afternoons I sometimes sat on the docks and watched Coleman casting his weighted net in a wide arc across the waters behind the building, catching mullet by the dozen. I'd always loved the smell of docks—the combination of diesel and freshly caught fish."

Mary, Coleman, and Fritz

Courtesy of Mary L. Trump.

"Dad's apartment in West Palm was larger and brighter than anywhere he had ever lived. When Fritz and I first visited, the boat—a nineteen-foot skiff with a sixty-horsepower Mercury outboard that he named Sundance Kid after his favorite movie—was waiting in its slip, tied to the dock as promised. There were also matching red windbreakers he'd had embroidered with the boat's name in white thread on one side and ours on the other."

Courtesy of Mary L. Trump.

"I excelled at heavy-weather sailing, when containing the power of the wind felt like a battle, the sails tightly trimmed as I pushed the bow as close to the wind as possible, the boat almost perpendicular to the sea. I loved the sudden rush of sound as the bow crossed the wind and the sails snapped full on the other side when coming about, or pulling the tiller to windward and, in one motion, letting the sheets slide through our hands until the jib and mainsail reached their farthest point, the sudden hush of the wind at our backs."

CCSC c. 1980, crewing for my friend, the best sailor at camp

Courtesy of Mary L. Trump.

"*Spring [at Walker's] brought possibilities. The air was thin and the April light spread through it, bright and sharp, with a clarity I hadn't felt in a long time. As I walked from one building to the next on my way to classes or the gym or my room, music blared from open dorm windows—a weird mélange of classic rock and whatever was in the Top 40—and it was easier out in the open to feel like I belonged, even if the feeling was illusory.*"

Courtesy of Mary L. Trump.

"*I flew out of my shoe. When I looked behind me, my far-too-expensive three-inch heel was jammed between two cobblestones a few feet from the entrance to the East Wing of the White House. I hopped back to retrieve it and stood on one foot while I slipped it back on. As soon as I took my first step, I knew I was in trouble. The heel had been knocked off-center just enough to make me feel like I was walking at a slant.*

Off-balance and out of control was a perfect description for how I felt about spending the evening with my estranged family at the White House on this April night in 2017."

"In his speech at the dining room table in the residential dining room, Robert outdid himself. As he droned on, referring to his older brother as 'Mr. President' at every turn, my contempt for him grew."

Robert Trump

"I brought a fraud suit against Donald, Robert, and Maryanne as the executors of my grandfather's estate, based on information from the New York Times *investigation. A year later, Donald sued me for $100 million."*

Donald, Elizabeth, Maryanne, and Robert

"I regretted my decision to attend the birthday party for my aunts Maryanne and Elizabeth almost as soon as I accepted the invitation."

———————

When we pulled up in the limo to the Jamaica Hospital entrance, Dad was waiting outside despite the bitter cold of the day, as if he were determined to make things worse. His trouser cuffs bagged around his ankles and his thin coat, hanging off his shoulders, flapped around him as he approached the car. My mother, her two friends, and I took up all the seats in the back. When Dad opened the back door—George hadn't even gotten out of the car to open it for him, as he customarily did for his passengers—he saw there wasn't enough room for him. He slammed the door shut and stalked to the front passenger-side door without saying a word.

I'd seen Dad angry only a handful of times, usually when he was disappointed (like the time we went to the movies to see what he thought was a rerelease of *Lawrence of Arabia* but was, instead, *The Wind and the Lion*—a very different movie), or when he was worried that he might be in trouble with his father. This was different. He seethed with a rage that felt active and ready to blow but that also covered something deeper and worse—a profound sense of hurt.

From where I sat in the back seat, I could see his face, pale and miserable, in profile, his jaw clenched. A shiver passed through him, as much, I thought, from the rage as from the cold. My mother and her friends chatted as if there weren't a cadaverous, deathly ill man—her ex-husband, the father of her children—two feet away. I did what had become habit by then: I stared out the window at the slick, grey streets and imagined I was somewhere, anywhere, else.

By the time we got to Columbia-Presbyterian nearly an hour later, Dad had fallen into a deep, exhausted sleep and could barely shake himself awake. Mom went in to the admissions

desk to let them know he was there and came out with an attendant pushing a wheelchair. It took a while to rouse Dad, and he
needed to be lifted into the chair. I followed him inside.

I'd seen Dad sick, jaundiced, drunk, and passed out. This
was an unfamiliar kind of vulnerability, and it frightened me.
After the admissions nurse checked him in, an orderly came to
take him to his room. As I watched his wheelchair recede down
the hall, I felt a momentary panic.

When we got back in the limo, my mother asked George if
he could take us to the Metropolitan Museum of Art, which had
been our original destination.

"Oh, no, Linda," George said. "Mr. Trump would never allow
that." He dropped us at the nearest subway station.

It was beginning to dawn on me that nothing these people did
ever made any sense, that there was something deeply out of
sync about the way my family operated. I wondered why my
father hadn't had the surgery in Miami, why he hadn't gone
straight from the airport to the hospital where the surgery was
going to be performed, why he hadn't been transported in an
ambulance. And, much more troubling than anything else, why
hadn't we stayed with him?

33

Two years earlier, Dad had come to the Highlander for dinner—a rare event in the seven years since my parents had divorced—to tell us he was planning to move to West Palm Beach, a town along the same stretch of coast as Fort Lauderdale, where my mother's father and stepmother, Violet, still lived. My grandmother, Mary Clapp, had died in 1967, and Mike had married Violet, a widow from Kalamazoo, the following year.

Dad told us about the apartment he found on the Intracoastal Waterway—it had a dock instead of a backyard—and he promised to get us a boat. The good moments had become fewer and farther between since his move to Sunnyside Towers, so this was an encouraging change. His optimism was contagious, and he exuded so much confidence and hope that, for a while, we all believed he could turn things around.

Dad's apartment in West Palm was larger and brighter than anywhere he had ever lived. When Fritz and I first visited, the boat—a nineteen-foot skiff with a sixty-horsepower Mercury outboard that he named *Sundance Kid* after his favorite movie—was waiting in its slip, tied to the dock as promised. There were also matching red windbreakers he'd had embroidered with the boat's name in white thread on one side and ours on the other.

I'd never before spent more than a night or two with Dad, and staying with him for a week or two at a time gave us a chance to get into a rhythm. Dad's aunt Joan, one of Gam's older sisters, lived nearby with her husband, Vic, and we saw them at least once or twice whenever we visited. We either went to their house for a meal or Dad took us to their favorite restaurant, a cavernous hall that catered to senior citizens and had dinner theater on the weekends.

Joan had immigrated to New York from Scotland in the early 1920s and met Vic when she was a domestic servant and he was a footman. By the time my grandmother had followed her over in 1930, Joan and Vic were already married. They never had children, but Vic, a man with a large, bald head and weak chin who favored blue dinner jackets and high-waisted polyester pants, knew how to make us kids laugh. Aunt Joan, the more reserved of the two, lit up whenever Uncle Vic pulled quarters from our ears or fashioned a mouse out of one of the restaurant's cloth napkins and somehow managed to make it squeak and jump across the table.

Dad was so comfortable with them, I assumed he'd spent a lot of time with them when he was growing up. Uncle Vic was such a warm, sweet man; he could not have been more different from Fred Trump, and I wondered sometimes what life would have been like if he had been my grandfather.

Dad befriended another airline pilot who lived in the same building, who offered to help him get his pilot's license renewed. In the meantime, Dad got a job navigating a boat for a well-off older man who owned a forty-five-foot Hatteras.

As we had been at the apartment in Sunnyside, we were often left on our own, but now we had a boat, some fishing rods, and a friend in the building, a boy named Coleman who was only a year or two older than I was.

The three of us spent a lot of time on the boat together, but on quiet afternoons I sometimes sat on the docks and watched Coleman casting his weighted net in a wide arc across the waters behind the building, catching mullet by the dozen.

I'd always loved the smell of docks—the combination of diesel and freshly caught fish. Dad taught me how to scale and gut fish like an expert when we were in Montauk. I loved posing with my catch, usually striped bass but sometimes bluefish, sliding my small fingers between their gills to hold them up for the camera. I wasn't particularly interested in catching mullet; it seemed like a waste and didn't present the same kind of challenge as the deep-sea fishing we did in Montauk. But there was a poetry to the casting of that wide circular net and a rhythmic physicality to hauling it against the weight of a dozen writhing fish and the pull of the water.

Dad picked up a couple of sturdy used bikes for us. After a long day on the water or on the docks, Fritz and I rode across town to the Cumberland Farms store, where we stocked up on Dubble Bubble and eggnog, which we happily chewed and drank together in the Florida heat.

34

S pring break was coming to a close, and we were heading
back to New York a couple of days early for Donald and
Ivana's wedding. Dad's tuxedo hung on the back of his bedroom
door, and he'd pulled out the suitcases to remind us we needed
to pack. Our flight out of the Fort Lauderdale airport was early
the following morning, and he didn't want to leave the packing
to the last minute.

Fritz and Coleman had ridden to the park to play basketball,
but I hadn't been in the mood to tag along, so I spent the last
afternoon sitting at the edge of the dock throwing stones. Half
the boat slips were empty. The boats that remained bumped
lightly against the pilings whenever the wake of a yacht reached
us from the Intracoastal.

Dad came down looking for us. When he saw Coleman's
mullet net, he asked if it had been rinsed off—it bothered him
when people didn't take care of their tackle. I said it had, and he
sat down next to me. He was wearing sunglasses, so I couldn't
see his eyes, but he seemed upset about something.

He lit a cigarette and waited, as if trying to figure something
out, then asked suddenly, "Want to take the boat out?"

I didn't, really. I'd spent the morning riding my bike and an
hour watching Coleman casting his net, and I'd just been about
to go inside. But I didn't want to say no. It was our last day, after
all, and I liked watching Dad drive—it always settled him. But
he surprised me and threw me the keys.

"OK, all yours," he said.

I got behind the wheel, and he released the line from the
cleat and pushed us off. The shadows were lengthening across

the inlet, but when I turned into the Intracoastal, the afternoon light shone silver as it reflected off the scales of fish that jumped through the crests of the waves.

Dad lit another cigarette and gazed out over the bow. He and I didn't talk much anymore, partly because he always seemed to have a lot on his mind but also because I had gotten quiet. In the past, our conversations had largely consisted of me asking questions, and I didn't do that much anymore. I think my serious turn baffled him, but he took it in stride, and that day I think he was happy to sit next to me in silence while I maneuvered the boat from the Intracoastal into the open water of the Atlantic and gunned the engine.

When we got back to the apartment, Fritz and Coleman were watching a baseball game and throwing a Nerf football across the living room, all sugared up after their run to Cumberland Farms on their way back from the park.

Dad reminded us we needed to pack. Coleman took the hint and left. I followed Dad into his room to get my suitcase. I noticed his tuxedo was gone and figured he'd already put his bag in the car.

After dinner, instead of staying to watch TV with us, Dad said he had some calls to make and went into his room. Fritz and I looked at each other and realized we weren't going to see him again that night. We packed while *The Honeymooners* played in the background, then got ready for bed. It was my turn to take the couch, so we moved the coffee table and spread Fritz's sheet and cotton blanket on the floor. I turned the light off, but we kept the TV on. I stayed awake until the white noise lulled me to sleep.

35

We'd been relegated to Siberia again. I don't know if the seating arrangements would have been any different if Dad had been there, but, as he told us on the way to the airport, there had been a change in plans: He wasn't going to be Donald's best man. He wasn't, in fact, going to be at the wedding at all. Uncle Vic had been ill for a few months, and the day before our flight back to New York, my grandfather told Dad he needed to stay in West Palm Beach to take care of him and Aunt Joan.

We had recently had dinner at their house, and although it was true that Uncle Vic was ill, the two of them could easily have managed without Dad for two days. The transparent lie would have bothered me more, but on the way home from the airport Mom broke the news to us that our cat Fluffy had died while we were away. Everything else was driven out of my head.

During the wedding ceremony the following day at Marble Collegiate Church, my mother wrapped her arm around my shoulder as I cried quietly. The reception afterward was held at the 21 Club, a once fashionable, old-school restaurant in midtown with a line of lawn jockeys arrayed along the outside stairs. When my mother realized we were seated at the second cousins' table, she withdrew into herself, rigid with resentment, my grief instantly forgotten.

Fritz had gone to sit with our cousin David at the table where my grandparents and Maryanne, Elizabeth, and Rob sat, so I was left to myself. Under normal circumstances, I would have tried to distract or console my mother all night, as I often did at family gatherings, but I didn't have it in me; my despair over Fluffy's death was too great.

As soon as I was sure nobody was paying attention (and nobody was), I started to sob into my napkin. The waiters put plates of food in front of me and took them away untouched.

Then I sensed somebody standing next to me. "Was it something I said?" an unfamiliar voice said.

I looked up, my eyes wet and red from crying. A man with a generous mustache, balding head, and pale skin smiled at me. In response to my look of confusion, he said, "That was a stupid question, wasn't it? I just wanted to see if you were OK."

I tried to smile but started crying again. He took the napkin out of my hand and gave me a clean one.

"Is it OK if I sit down?"

I nodded again.

He sat and lit a cigarette, blowing the smoke over my head. "Did something happen?" He sounded concerned, and surveyed the room as if looking for whoever might have hurt me. "Is somebody bothering you?"

I shook my head but couldn't yet talk.

He leaned his elbow against the table and said, "I'm Malcolm. Your dad is my cousin, so your grandmother is my mom's sister—your great-aunt Kate." Gam talked to her sister Kate almost every day, so I knew who she was. "I'm sorry we've never met before," Malcolm said, "but we live in Canada, way on the California side." He gestured vaguely and I imagined how far that was.

"I'm really sorry Freddy couldn't be here. Your dad's such a good guy. In fact, he's the person I wanted to hang out with tonight."

He was starting to get my attention. Before I knew it, I had calmed down enough to tell him about Fluffy, how heartbroken I was, the last-minute change in Dad's plans.

Malcolm asked me to explain, and when I did, he looked

troubled. He took a sip of his drink. "Your dad likes Florida, though?"

I told him about the apartment with the dock, our little boat, Dad's job, and Uncle Vic's illness. Whenever the waiter came by, Malcolm put his empty glass on the tray and asked for another.

Malcolm told me about the time Dad had flown him out to Montauk on a seaplane and how they'd anchored the plane next to the beach at Gurney's and ate steamers and lobster on the deck.

I forgot all about Mom and the seating arrangements. For a few minutes, I even forgot to be sad.

Before I knew it, the reception was over and people started heading to the coat check.

"Mary," Malcolm said, "it was so good to spend time with you. Just between you and me"—he lowered his voice—"when I found out your dad wasn't going to be here, I was kind of dreading it." He smiled at me and held out his hand. "I hope we see each other again."

Instead of shaking his hand, I hugged him. He seemed surprised, but he hugged me back. "And I'm going to call your dad."

That Christmas, my mother planned for us to visit her father, Mike, and Violet in Fort Lauderdale. I assumed we'd see my father, too, but when I was at the House one Sunday a couple of weeks before winter break, my grandfather and Rob, who had come in from the city for Gam's waffle breakfast, were standing in the foyer talking.

I heard my grandfather say, "That poor slob." Rob just shook his head. "He didn't know you were going down there for Christmas, and he's coming up here," he said to me.

This seemed to amuse my grandfather greatly, but I didn't know why. I walked away wondering why the arrangements couldn't be changed. My grandfather's words, "That poor slob," stuck with me.

36

The boat Dad piloted for Mr. Dreyer was merely for show, and it didn't take long for him to feel unfulfilled. It was supposed to be a temporary gig while he tried to get cleared to fly again, but that never happened. Mr. Dreyer took the Hatteras out infrequently, and even then, it was only for quick jaunts with his equally elderly friends, or to cruise with his grown children and grandchildren along the shore. There were no daylong expeditions in search of marlin or other sport fish. Dad thought it was a waste of the boat and his expertise as both a pilot and fisherman.

The last couple of times we'd been to Montauk, when Dad still lived in Sunnyside, we'd hopped onto an open boat to catch fluke, along with dozens of other passengers with rented rods who had no idea what they were doing. But when I was younger, Dad borrowed boats from his friends—the serious kind of fishing boats that he had once owned—and drove us miles offshore chasing schools of striped bass or bluefish while he tried to hook something bigger and, for him, more challenging.

We had no experiences like that in West Palm Beach. Our boat was too small to do the kind of sportfishing Dad liked, and we didn't have the right equipment anyway. We had water skis, but, although the sixty-horsepower outboard had enough power to get us upright, I never managed to drop a ski, and without being able to slalom, I got bored with it.

Over spring break in 1978, my mother and a friend of hers who also had kids at Kew-Forest planned a trip to Disney World, and Dad invited everybody to stay for a few days at his apartment before we went to Orlando. He had stopped working by then. Uncle Vic had died four months after Donald's wedding, and that hadn't helped. Dad was desperate in more ways than anybody could fathom, and when he found himself alone with my mother, he drunkenly suggested to her that they get back together. She said no, and then laughed about it later.

Dad continued to have dinner with Aunt Joan at least once a week, but her depression deepened in the months after Uncle Vic's death, and it was hard on both of them. During our last visit (which we didn't know at the time was going to be our last visit), the four of us had a particularly grim meal in the near-empty dinner theater restaurant.

Dad was out of sorts and Aunt Joan barely said a word, which left it up to Fritz and me to manufacture conversation. Fritz told Aunt Joan about our latest exploits with Coleman. We'd taken the boat out a couple of days earlier and had accidentally hooked a grouper—a fish that can weigh hundreds of pounds—and it had almost pulled the bow of our boat under the surface before we cut the line. Fritz made it sound much more dramatic and exciting than it actually was, but in truth, we were embarrassed because we should have known better.

After a beat, Fritz said, philosophically, "It just occurred to me: Coleman is only fourteen. Shouldn't his name be Coal Minor?"

Nobody said a word.

Dad looked down at his almost-empty glass and swirled the ice around. I could tell he was debating whether to order another one. Aunt Joan looked wounded as she sat there pushing her food around with her fork.

It took a minute, but when I got the joke, I started laughing despite the clear signs nobody else thought it was funny.

Dad raised his arm and flagged down the waiter. In three months, he'd be back in New York for good.

37

As we grew older, and especially after my cousin David went to college and Aunt Maryanne moved out of Queens into Manhattan, we spent much less time at the House. After Dad was released from the hospital, I visited as often as I could, but when I turned my bike in to the driveway, I knew only he and my grandmother would be there. The House felt like an abandoned relic.

Gam was usually in the kitchen reading a magazine or talking on the phone. Before I went upstairs, she would pour a Coke into a glass with ice and say, "Bring this to your father."

Dad's surgery had been a success, but over the course of the first two weeks of his recuperation, back in the Cell, it was hard to tell—he wasn't just weak, he was utterly depleted. I'd sit with him for a while, changing the station of the transistor radio on his bedside table if he asked, or simply watching him. He lay there with his eyes closed or with his face to the wall as if he didn't want to be seen, a sense of hopelessness radiating off him.

Then I rode back home to another parent who was barely functioning. When Dad had lived in Sunnyside Towers, spending time with him often felt like walking into a game of Russian roulette. Now his dark moods, on the one hand, and the durability of my mother's depression and neglect, on the other, became the magnetic poles of my existence.

I don't know why Dad's return to New York had such a big impact on my mother. Maybe his being back in the House— a place he'd arguably been trying to escape even as he repeatedly and sometimes voluntarily returned—reminded her that she, too, was paralyzed by the same forces. She could no more escape the Trump vortex than he could, still living in the Trump-owned apartment she hated. Her hatred of it came as much from the way she perceived her treatment by the superintendent and porters and doormen who worked there as from the reality that there was nowhere else she could reasonably afford to go with the limited funds she received for alimony and child support.

There was always something wrong with the apartment. The pipes were rusty and the water that came out of the taps was brown. We had infestations of ants. Cockroaches, which were a feature of living in New York City, sometimes infiltrated our food supply. Not only had the air conditioners been installed improperly, but the windows in my brother's room hadn't been properly sealed and the wood frame completely rotted through; during the winter, cold air blew through unimpeded, causing Fritz, like my father more than fifteen years earlier, to get pneumonia.

When Mom was finally able to get the building superintendent to take a look, he said he'd see what he could do. After a week passed and she still hadn't heard from him, we went to his office. When she asked when she could expect the window to be repaired, he shook his head. "Mr. Trump" hadn't authorized him to replace the windows, he said. The best he could do was cover the old ones with plastic sheeting.

Fritz was sent to Florida to stay with my maternal grandparents in Fort Lauderdale for three weeks. When he returned, my grandfather Mike accompanied him and fixed the windows with plywood and Spackle using tools he brought with him.

Mom's inability to get attended to made her crazy. It was bad enough that my grandfather owned the building, but it was worse than that—we actually paid rent (at a discounted amount, but rent just the same). Even worse, although I doubt he knew it at the time, and I certainly didn't, my father owned 15 percent of the building.

Once he started high school, Fritz was rarely home on Friday or Saturday nights. If our mother was in a fair mood, he took her car keys and left without comment. But if she was experiencing one of her increasingly frequent and deep depressions, he would say over his shoulder as he walked out the door, "You need to stay with Mom." As my big brother, he had sway over me, and I obeyed. On those nights, regardless of what I might have had planned—if somebody in my grade was having a party or one of my friends had invited me for a sleepover—I, as the younger child, had to stay home to watch over my mother. She and I sat next to each other on the love seat in the den watching television until she went to bed. Neither of us spoke a word.

There had always been an undercurrent of fear in the apartment (very different in quality from the fear the arguments between her and my father sparked). My love for my mother was so complete, I didn't recognize that she was the source of it.

She came to my games at school. When she visited me at camp, she invited my friends to join us for dinner. Everybody who met her under those circumstances found her personable and friendly. But when I invited friends to our apartment for a sleepover, I always regretted it. She was often in a dark mood in the morning, which made her quiet and withdrawn. My friends might be loud and wake her up. She wasn't a screamer, and she wasn't violent. She slapped me maybe twice over the course of my life for some infraction I'd committed, but that was all. And yet I was terrified of upsetting her. I adored her so much that her silence toward me was excruciating. My father's leaving—and subsequent frequent abdication of parental responsibility—made me even more grateful that my mother had stuck by us.

When she suffered, I suffered. It was my responsibility to comfort her. She wouldn't have had to endure the indignities of attending family events with her former in-laws if it weren't for me. Sometimes it felt as if my very existence was the thing that hurt her.

When I was in second grade, one of my best friends slept over. The next morning, I decided the two of us should make pancakes, which we started to do while my mother slept. It seemed like such a wonderful idea at the time, to surprise Mom with breakfast. But as soon as I heard her get out of bed and surveyed the mess I'd made—the broken eggshells, the flour on the floor, and the spilled pancake batter—I was seized with panic. I picked the bowl of batter up from the counter, climbed down from the stepladder, and told my friend to follow me.

The two of us hid behind the couch. I hoped that if my mother couldn't find me, she wouldn't realize I was the culprit.

For fear of making her angry, I learned how to restrain my impulse to be a kid who, on occasion, did spontaneously normal stupid kid things. Her anger was shot through with a deep sense of disappointment, and whenever she expressed it—even quietly—her sense of having been grievously wounded cut right through me. Life had been unfair to her, and I was making everything worse. I came to believe her quiet rage had such power, it would obliterate me if I ever got in its path.

Issues like the knots in my hair, or my shirt missing a button, or the hem of my kilt having come undone, which my teachers had never mentioned to me before, were raised as problems I needed to solve.

Every night after I showered, I massaged conditioner into my hair and left it in for an hour hoping that that would make it easier to comb the knots out; it didn't. One night as I was falling asleep, I was seized with the idea that my mother was going to come into my room in the middle of the night with a pair of scissors and cut off my hair. The terror about this was abject and unreasoning. I hadn't been as scared, at least consciously, of anything since I read *In Cold Blood*. I began to stay up late no matter how tired I was, just in case.

Between that and my weekends at home watching over my mother, I wanted to be home as little as possible during the week. Mornings were easy: I'd been taking the bus or subway to school since fifth grade, so I could leave before my mother even woke up and while Fritz was still in the shower so he couldn't demand I come home after school. In eighth grade my friends and I started to meet at the candy store next to the Queens Boulevard subway station, a couple of blocks from school, so I didn't even bother eating breakfast at home anymore, opting instead to grab a bagel at the bagel place next to the candy store or a candy bar and a can of soda or Country Time lemonade. The main reason we met at the candy store, though, was the video games. If we got there early enough, we could put our quarters on the machines and reserve them before anybody else showed up. My friends and I met an hour and a half before school started to play Asteroids, Space Invaders, Missile Command, Crash, and Ms. Pac-Man. We played a lot and eventually got so good that we either cracked the game's code and could make the game last indefinitely or could make one quarter last over an hour, which infuriated anybody else who was waiting for their turn.

But this required funds I didn't always have, which was enough impetus for me to put my fear aside. While I worried about my friends waking her when they stayed over, the truth was my mother slept so deeply that I could go into her bedroom and walk right past her as she lay in bed. She kept an envelope full of singles, fives, tens, and a few twenties in the top drawer of her dresser, and when I was short of money, I stole as much as I needed for the next couple of days.

My mother kept track of the funds by writing a column of numbers, including additions and subtractions, in pencil on the outside of the envelope, so in order to make sure I got away with my petty theft, I subtracted the amount I took in as close an approximation of her handwriting as possible. Sometimes it was too dark to see in the early morning before the sun came up, so I had to remember to take care of it when I got back from school.

I tried to find any reason I could to stay out late as well. If there was an after-school event—a dance, a play, the end-of-year musical, a game—I volunteered, or spectated, or played. If there was no legitimate reason to stay at school after hours, and the video games at the candy store had been monopolized by the older kids, my friends and I went to a pool hall on Queens Boulevard past Metropolitan Avenue—the only females and the only people under fifty by over three decades—and rented a table for a couple of hours: "the glorious results of a misspent youth."

38

It took a long time, but once Dad was on his feet after his surgery and able to go downstairs—with the assistance of Gam's electric chairlift, which my grandfather had installed when her repeated bone breaks made climbing the stairs impossible—his spirits improved. He looked better than he had in a long time, not only because he was recovering well from the surgery, but because he hadn't had a drink or a cigarette in over two months. He talked about getting his own place again, maybe even going back to Florida. He didn't get into specifics. He may have had a plan, but he wasn't ready to share it.

39

This time I was awakened by a pain that was both sharp and unfamiliar, not heavy and dull like asthma; and the pain, though it was located in my stomach, not my lungs, still felt dangerous.

What was happening? Did I have appendicitis? Was it something I ate?

For dinner, we'd had pizza from Nino's, on the corner of Hillside Avenue and Midland Parkway, just a few blocks from the House. It was a long way to go for pizza, but it was the best, and Nino, an old-school twirler of pizza dough, always gave me a small fountain soda while I waited. I'd had two slices of our usual—mushroom, meatball, and onion—which I ate while we watched a rerun of *Planet of the Apes*.

I pulled my knees up toward my chest to see if that would help, but it only made the pain worse. I tried to turn onto my side but couldn't. I looked down at my belly—it was so distended that it looked like I'd swallowed a basketball, which freaked me out. I screamed for my mother.

"It's my stomach," I told her when she opened my door. "Something's really wrong."

She walked over to my bed and I pulled down the sheet to show her my stomach. She pressed it with her finger.

"I'll be right back," she said.

Within two minutes, she was back, fully clothed. It couldn't have been much past two in the morning, but my mother did something extraordinary—she took me to the hospital. If only I could scream when I couldn't breathe.

They diagnosed me with a severe case of gastroenteritis and

admitted me almost immediately. Two hours after I arrived, I was settled into a room in the adult ward with no roommates and a stomach tube up my nose. It would be a few days before they'd let me go home, but by the next day, I already felt surprisingly well. I could read and do homework and talk on the phone with friends.

On the third day of my stay, two boys from school, Ben and Andrew, stopped by for a visit. They were two grades ahead of me and I had a crush on Ben, so I was shy at first and a little self-conscious (it's hard to entertain when you have a tube up your nose), but they quickly put me at ease as if we were equals, even though I was a mere freshman.

And then Dad stumbled in. I hadn't seen him in weeks, since the last time I'd been to the House and found him in the attic, drunk and smoking a cigarette only four months out from his open-heart surgery. He'd once told me that, after he was hospitalized with a bad case of pneumonia when I was little, his doctor had made it clear that if he had another drink he'd die. I'd lost count of how many times he'd fallen off the wagon, but even so, given the seriousness of the open-heart surgery and how well he'd been doing, I was shocked at the latest regression. He waved loosely to Ben and Andrew, walked over to me, and sat awkwardly on the edge of my bed.

"Hey, sweetie pie. Looking good!" He pointed to the stomach tube. He placed a brown paper bag on my lap and said, "You know what I was thinking about on the way over here? Guys, do you know what I was thinking?"

"What was that, Mr. Trump?" Ben asked politely. Both he and Andrew looked as if they'd rather be anywhere else.

He looked at me now, his eyes red. He smelled of alcohol and stale cigarette smoke. "I was thinking just how lucky you are. There are kids all over the world so much worse off than you."

I didn't feel particularly lucky, but I said nothing.

He pointed at the bag. "I got this for you," he slurred. "Looked everywhere to find the perfect gift."

I tentatively reached for it.

"Oh, come on," he said impatiently. "Open it up." He seemed eager for me to see the present he'd bought for me. He turned the bag upside down and a heavy, faceted piece of Lucite fell onto the sheets and almost rolled off the side of the bed.

I grabbed it and held it up. The Lucite was on a small faux-marble trophy stand, and I could see something embedded in it that I couldn't quite identify.

"It's a piece of horse shit," Dad said loudly.

"Wow. Thanks, Dad." I looked straight at him with all of the hatred I felt in that moment.

He didn't notice, and beamed at his own cleverness.

Dad's gifts had often been questionable. He gave me a copy of W. C. Fields's book *I Never Met a Kid I Liked*, with a blue felt-tip inscription in his loopy handwriting that read, "I love you more than Fields, Daddy." I struggled to understand what that meant. I love you more than I love Fields? I love you more than Fields loves you? Either way, it wasn't really saying much—unless he really loved Fields a lot.

But there was no ambiguity here. Far beyond the embarrassment of being humiliated in front of my friends, for the first time in my life, I felt his contempt.

Dad tried to get up from the bed and slipped. He started laughing. Before he hit the floor, Ben ran over and grabbed Dad by the elbow. "That's OK, Mr. Trump, I got you." He steered Dad toward the door and said to me and Andrew, "Be right back." The two of us remained frozen in silence until Ben came back. When he did, he said cheerfully, "All set. He's going to be fine."

I kept my eyes down. I couldn't look at either one of them, just as I couldn't prevent the blush that spread across my cheeks.

"We're going to head out. Keep getting better and we'll see you at school in a couple of days," Ben said.

I didn't think I'd ever go back to school again.

"Bye, Mary. Feel better," Andrew said.

I didn't respond. And then they were gone.

40

By the time Fritz left for college, my sense of obligation to either of my parents had worn thin. The task of negotiating the difficulties of adolescence on top of the strange dynamics between my divorced parents (she hated him but couldn't let go of her feelings; he wouldn't say a word against her and withstood her diatribes against him like a stoic who had it coming); the worsening of Dad's alcoholism; my mother's intractable depression; and my regular and increasingly debilitating asthma attacks together wore me out.

These beats became the background noise of my life, like a repeating *Flintstones* backdrop—house, rock, dinosaur. If you wait long enough, another one will come streaming by. The only way I could control the cadence was to avoid my parents as much as possible.

When Dad had recovered sufficiently from his surgery, my grandfather, perhaps as a way to derail any other plans Dad might have had, told him he needed to start working again and offered him a job at Trump Management. Donald had moved to an office in Manhattan, so Dad considered it. But it turned out the job being offered wasn't in the office on Avenue Z. Instead, it was a job working on a maintenance crew at Trump Village, the same development whose construction sixteen years earlier, in 1963, had prompted Dad to quit Trump Management and become a professional pilot. Dad spent his days stripping paint, raking leaves, or fixing broken toilets—all things he'd done during summers working for Trump Management when he was in high school.

The job humiliated him, and that, of course, was the point as far as my grandfather was concerned—that's what made it enjoyable, seeing his oldest son so dependent and beaten down that he would take the scraps and be grateful for them. Dad didn't say anything to me about it one way or the other. But that's when he started drinking and smoking again.

I stayed away from home even on the weekends now that my brother wasn't around to tell me what to do. It wasn't only the oppressive silence or the walking on eggshells; I'd learned that after my mother told me to get in bed next to her when I had an asthma attack, and I sat up waiting for the sun to rise until she finally took me to the hospital, she was awake the whole time.

"Every time she takes a breath, the bed shakes," she told a friend during a lunch we were having at the Bloomingdale's café, as if that were a feat to marvel at instead of a reality that should have spurred her into action.

Now when I went into my mother's room—when the rescue inhaler had failed yet again—I didn't even bother to wake her up; I simply took my place in the bed next to her and left her undisturbed. When she woke up in the morning, she'd know immediately that it was time to take me to the hospital. It saved me the trouble of being reminded yet again that she didn't care enough to do anything.

I got up earlier and earlier on the weekdays, in part because my friends and I started meeting at the candy store at six thirty, but also because I needed at least half an hour to comb the knots out of my hair, which I'd finally figured out how to do. It was one small way to make sophomore year slightly less horrible. Whatever energy I had left went to keeping up the pretense that I was on top of things, that I was in control, while denying that life was shifting into the terrifying and shaky realm of rivalry, misunderstanding, conflict, and insecurity from which I'd been almost entirely immune before high school.

I spent inordinate amounts of time dreaming about camp, writing letters to my camp friends, and counting down the days until we drove to Brewster for opening day. Over the years, mostly because of camp, I'd developed a certain level of self-confidence, and I could no longer back it up. The distance between me and my friends had been growing for years because of the secrets I had to keep. Most of the time I felt utterly alone.

41

In a picture my father took when my parents were first married, my mother is eating a hot dog and my grandfather stands just behind her wearing a suit and tie.

Before I saw this photograph, I didn't realize there had ever been family barbecues at all—we'd never had one—but I was also surprised to see where it had been held. It was easy to forget, because nobody ever opened the door at the far end of the library, but there was a small covered porch that, despite the wrought iron furniture that still sat out there, nobody used—it was just dead leaves and tumbleweeds and eerie silence. This porch was on the side of the House that always felt like no-man's-land, with a wide bed of ivy along the neighbor's property line and a grass path that led from the backyard to a small gate opening onto the front yard. There was something vaguely creepy about it.

There was no indication that it had ever been a place where the family gathered.

Easter and Mother's Day (which was always combined with my grandmother's birthday), celebrated at my grandparents' country club, North Hills, and my grandfather's birthday at Peter Luger Steak House in Williamsburg, Brooklyn, were the only occasions we got together as a family outside of the House.

There was never a time when Maryanne, Donald, Elizabeth, or Robert spent Thanksgiving or Christmas with their spouses' families. Yet we never did anything else as a family: It was different for Fritz, who was connected to the family in a more direct way because our cousin David was his best friend. Once the two of them left for college, I was on my own.

The formal dining room in my grandparents' house was furnished with a mahogany sideboard and matching table just long enough to accommodate my grandparents, my aunts and uncles and their spouses, my mother, me, Fritz, and David. The sunken living room, at the other end of the foyer, had the same heavy velvet drapes and densely woven taupe carpet. Despite the House's perch high on a hill, unobstructed view of the sky, and southern exposure, both rooms were constantly in shadow, as if they were windowless.

My grandparents sat at opposite ends of the dining table, Gam nearest the kitchen, with me tucked in next to her. Donald sat at my grandfather's right hand, which placed us as far away from each other as we could be. All the power resided at that end of the table. The absurd imbalance of it became even more obvious on those rare occasions when Dad joined us, and when in the late seventies Maryanne started bringing her new boyfriend, John Barry, a savvy and successful commercial litigator and white-collar criminal-defense attorney from New Jersey who counted Donald among his clients. Maryanne sat to my grandfather's left. Dad sat next to me.

Maryanne had been on her way to obtaining a PhD in public policy when she met David Desmond, another Columbia grad student with big dreams but no discernible way of fulfilling them. She dropped out of school after receiving her master's in order to marry him, even though they barely knew each other. They moved immediately into one of my grandfather's buildings only a few blocks from the House.

David was unemployed for long stretches of time, and

Maryanne spent her days typing up his résumés and cover letters while he sat nearby "overseeing" her and drinking from a bottle of Old Grand-Dad. Other than a job as a parking lot attendant my grandfather had given him, David was out of work for five years. The combination of frustration and drunkenness often made him violent; when he found out Maryanne had been applying to law schools, he threw their son, David, who was only thirteen at the time, out of the apartment. Until then, Maryanne had been scared to leave him, believing that marriage was supposed to be forever.

My grandmother knew about the problems in her eldest child's home life long before her grandson showed up at the House the day his father shoved him into the hallway and locked the door behind him, but she didn't make a fuss because, as Maryanne said, her mother wanted her "to have her pride." Gam kept Maryanne's family afloat with Crisco cans full of the dimes and quarters collected from Trump-building laundry machines. After Maryanne graduated from Hofstra Law School, she landed a job as an assistant US attorney with a paycheck of eleven thousand dollars a year, so those coins continued to come in handy.

Unencumbered by her now ex-husband, whom her siblings had openly mocked, Maryanne began to insert herself into every conversation Donald and my grandfather had. Many of them revolved around New York City real estate and politics, but they also included personal attacks on women the men found unattractive and grievances against anybody who didn't flatter Donald sufficiently. Maryanne knew all the players, all the deals, and all the politics inside out, even though most of it was outside of her purview as a prosecutor—she made sure to do her homework.

My mother's position at the table, and in the family, never changed, stuck as she was between the Scylla of her being required to attend family events and the Charybdis of nobody wanting her there. She believed she was doing it for us, but her presence only made things more awkward. And all she got for her trouble was dismissal and a trail of insulting Christmas presents.

42

On the morning of my sixteenth birthday, I waited for Dad on the sidewalk across the street from the Highlander. When he pulled up in his old Ford LTD, with its FCT vanity plate, I slid into the passenger seat. I hadn't seen him in a few weeks and he looked terrible. He'd missed a spot shaving, and his skin had the pallor of somebody who was seriously ill.

The last time I'd been to the House, Dad told me that Donald had agreed to let us have my birthday party in one of the small ballrooms at the Grand Hyatt. (This had been my mother's idea.) The Hyatt was a new hotel in midtown the success of which was being attributed—by Donald, his father, and a gullible New York media—to Donald, even though the only reasons it had been possible in the first place were my grandfather's deep pockets and even deeper connections to New York politicos.

I was shocked not only by Dad's appearance but also by how nervous he seemed. I knew he was there to give me my birthday present, but I didn't understand why he'd made this special trip, or why I had to meet him in the car like this. I was going to see him at the party, which was less than a week away, but he said he'd come to me and it wouldn't take long.

At the time, I was just starting to get into photography. I'd bought an Olympus OM-2 a few months earlier. I had asked my mother for an Olympus telephoto lens for my birthday, but I hadn't gotten it and assumed that was the end of it. The party was my big present.

Somehow, Dad knew better than to put my gift in a brown paper bag this time. He simply reached behind my seat and handed me the box. Here was the lens I had asked for, but a different brand. I'd done my research, so I knew one difference was the price—the one he gave me was significantly cheaper.

Before I could say anything, Dad tried to make his case. "Your mom told me you wanted the Olympus lens. I went to the camera store to ask about it, and they told me that that's a great lens, but they also recommended this one." He glanced over at me to get my reaction, but I looked down at my hands and didn't respond.

"The other one is like a BMW and this one is a Mercedes. They're both equally good." He lit a cigarette and his hand shook. He sounded desperate, and I hated him for it. I opened the car door and said, "Sure, Dad. Thanks for this." I waved the box sarcastically at him as I left the car and slammed the door.

My ability to be kind had finally short-circuited. I abandoned all expectations, becoming impervious to disappointment. When Dad didn't show up, I was relieved. As his moods got darker and more dangerous, I didn't flinch. When he seemed hopeless and beyond everything, I didn't care. I was ashamed of him and hoped he'd stay away. If he humiliated or scared me, I laughed it off.

I became cold and hard and utterly unlike myself.

Dad was wearing his madras blazer. His white shirt was crisp, and his black tie perfectly straight. There was a small cluster of round tables around the dance floor of the small Grand Hyatt party room, and he sat at one of them by himself, his legs crossed, smoking cigarette after cigarette, a check made out to Donald for renting us the space sitting on the table in front of him. Donald walked in, expansive about his new hotel, crowing about the fixtures to a roomful of teenagers who couldn't have cared less. He swanned around as if it were his grand opening, as if *he* were the host.

I paid no attention. It was the best birthday party I'd ever had. I didn't even notice when Dad left.

43

In an echo of my first day as a camper in 1971, I felt a little lonely and sad as I sat on my bunk at the beginning of my summer as a JC III. I'd just learned I'd be the only camper in my year. The Junior Counselor Training Program was like high school, and years were like grades: JC I the summer before freshman year, JC II the summer before sophomore, and so on. Prior to my arrival, I'd learned that my three closest camp friends in my year would not be returning. Now I discovered that no one else in my year had come back, either. There had never been a mass exodus like it before. I had a lot of friends who were both older and younger, but it wasn't the same.

They assigned me to the same cabin as the assistant counselors—the JC IVs—but it was a strange arrangement. The assistant counselors were split into two groups: each spent half the summer sleeping in my cabin and working at the day camp down the beach where the old boys' camp used to be. (The boys' camp had merged onto the far superior girls' campus to make a combined Cape Cod Sea Camp in 1975, not long before Fritz stopped going.) The other group lived as counselors in the cabins housing the younger kids. Halfway through the summer, just when I'd gotten close to the ACs in my cabin, the two groups swapped places, and I was bunking again with people most of whom I didn't know very well.

I worked harder than I ever had that summer. In order to progress through the ranks of the JC program, we had to declare majors; completing them required reaching a certain level of proficiency in your chosen discipline and completing teaching and maintenance hours (like cleaning and sighting rifles, splicing frayed line, or repairing the fletching on old arrows). Since I'd been there for ten years, I'd already reached or exceeded the proficiency levels for all five of my majors except sailing, which was the most demanding and time consuming of them.

It gave me something to work toward, and I worked as if I were fending something off as much as I was trying to succeed. Whether or not I was willing to admit it, the cracks in my confidence and self-esteem that had been forming for years had turned into fissures. I expended an enormous amount of energy trying to prevent that from having too much of an impact on my summer.

With the exception of low tides and my other responsibilities, I spent as much time as I could sailing. I was a good sailor but never as good as I wanted to be. Sailing, more than any of the other sports I focused on—like swimming or riflery—couldn't be set aside for ten months without losing a lot of your edge. It required a constant honing of instincts and an understanding of forces outside yourself.

My archery skills also degraded over the ten long months away from camp, but in the end, it was just me, my bow, an arrow, a target, and my own stillness, which I had become expert at controlling to one degree or another; it also helped that I knew how to be patient and how to hold my breath.

I excelled at heavy-weather sailing, when containing the power of the wind felt like a battle, the sails tightly trimmed as I pushed the bow as close to the wind as possible, the boat almost perpendicular to the sea. I loved the sudden rush of sound as the bow crossed the wind and the sails snapped full on the other side when coming about, or pulling the tiller to windward and, in one motion, letting the sheets slide through our hands until the jib and mainsail reached their farthest point, the sudden hush of the wind at our backs.

By the middle of the summer, I was exhausted and had a hard time getting up in the morning. I ticked off the days until I had to go home, filled with dread as the numbers got smaller.

Sometimes after dinner, if I had time, I went down to the beach as the sun was getting lower in the sky. I preferred it when the tide was out and I could walk straight out onto the flats and explore what the retreating water revealed. I never got bored of watching the dying light of the evening sun glance off the sandbars and tide pools.

On days when the clouds gathered and everything was shot through with the steel grey of a coming storm like weathered cedar shingles, or when the tide was too high to wander the beach, I sat on the dunes and wondered how the hell I was going to handle going home.

The summer before, I had written to my mother about transferring out of Kew-Forest to Horace Mann, a private school in the Bronx. It didn't go anywhere because the commute by public transportation was almost two hours each way and I would have had to rely on my mother. The drive wasn't bad, but during rush hour it likely would have been a nightmare. At the time, I still thought school, not home, was the problem, but after my brother left for college, I realized it was both.

When a camp friend of mine mentioned she was going to boarding school in the fall, the perfect solution presented itself. One of my camp counselors was a PE teacher and coach at the Ethel Walker School in Simsbury, Connecticut, and she encouraged me to apply there. I wrote home and told my mother about my plan. I asked her to put together a list of schools I might apply to, including Walker's, and asked her to request applications so I could get a start on them as soon as possible.

I don't know if she realized how serious I was until I sent her the completed applications and asked her to add my transcripts and medical records before sending them off. I was on a mission. I even wrote my father to give him a heads-up because he needed to talk to my grandfather about the tuition.

When camp ended for the season, I was sad, as always, and cried the whole way back to New York, but I believed there was a good chance I wouldn't be home for long. I knew it would be a stretch—I had less than three weeks until the semester started to find out if I'd been accepted to any schools, visit the campuses of those schools that had accepted me, and convince my grandfather to agree to it. But I might actually have a chance to start over.

Dad didn't respond to either of the letters I'd written to him from camp because, as I learned when I got home, he'd been in rehab again. The year and a half back in New York, and especially his living in the House, had taken their toll. It wasn't Donald's success that bothered my father—as far as he was concerned, there was never any competition between them and there never had been. It wasn't even their father's preference for Donald. Dad's friends had often commented on how enamored Fred seemed to be with Donald, but none of them understood it— Donald's charms were evident to nobody but Fred. The thing that broke my father in the end was a combination of Fred's disdain for him, Fred's need simultaneously to elevate Donald and to humiliate my father, and Dad's recognition that there was literally nothing he could do to change any of it.

Gam had called Maryanne sometime in July to tell her how concerned she was. It wasn't just the drinking and smoking— although obviously these created more concern in the wake of his open-heart surgery—but that Dad had started missing work and sometimes she could barely get him to wake up in the morning. The tension between my grandfather and his oldest son, and thus in the House, was worse than ever.

Without telling my father, Maryanne made arrangements to take him to the Carrier Clinic, a rehab facility in New Jersey. She drove to the House with John Barry, with whom she was living at the time, and begged her brother to try rehab one more time, for her sake if nothing else. By then, Dad had given up on the idea that anything could help him, but he was willing to go back into rehab for Maryanne even if he thought it was a waste of time. By then, Maryanne realized that Dad had already gotten helplessness in his bones; and Fred, who had a sociopath's joy in inflicting pain on other people, piled humiliation on top of it.

The twenty-eight days away was enough to dry Dad out, but it solved nothing, it changed nothing. After Maryanne picked him up at the end of his stay, she brought him straight back to the House as if none of them could possibly be bothered to find another way. When she checked on him the next day, Dad was already drinking again.

The drinking was a symptom, had always been a symptom, not only of the alcoholism but of his father's all-consuming disapproval of who he was. There was no way for Dad to escape the trap because none of them had any real interest in finding another solution. In the end, the House was the only place left for him to go.

The first time I saw Dad after I got home from camp, he looked better than he had two months earlier, but there were signs that all was not well. If I'd been paying attention, I might have been more alarmed by his loss of weight. He smoked almost constantly. My grandfather no longer let him smoke inside, so when I visited him at the House, we often sat on the steps of the porch in the backyard or, if my grandfather was home, we went for a drive in his car just so he could have a few cigarettes without getting in trouble. The familiar clink of bottles rolling around on the floor of the back seat also should have alerted me that all was not well, but I was too focused on getting away from home.

46

I was much more at ease than I had been before camp started. Some of the schools I'd applied to weren't taking new students so close to the new semester, but I'd been accepted to a few, including my first choice, which bolstered my confidence that I'd be gone by the beginning of September. Knowing that made it easier to spend time with my mother. Those days we spent on the road crisscrossing Connecticut and Massachusetts to visit campuses were the easiest we'd had together in a long time. The weather was late-summer perfect and as we drove, "Elton's Song" and "Believe It or Not" seemed to be on a constant loop on the radio. In the afternoons after my interviews, we explored the towns and shopped for fall clothes before checking in to a local motel.

When I was home, I spent as much time as I could with my Kew-Forest friends, knowing we probably wouldn't be at school together come September. We went to see the movie *Arthur* so many times we memorized large chunks of it. We drank whatever alcohol we could get our hands on and played Monopoly while listening to Pete Townshend and Billy Joel and Pat Benatar.

About ten days before the semester started, Walker's called to tell me I'd been accepted—there was no time to send a letter—but there was one problem: they didn't have room for me. As soon as I'd seen the curriculum and visited the sixty-acre campus with its outrageous facilities—soccer and softball fields instead of the gravel pit at Kew-Forest, tennis courts, horseback riding trails, and a state-of-the-art auditorium instead of a basketball court that doubled as one—I knew it was where I wanted to go.

I was crushed that I might have to decide between choosing a school I didn't like nearly as much or staying home.

Dad didn't want me to fall into the same trap Maryanne had fallen into. He wanted to encourage my ambition, not thwart it. "It's a good idea for you to get out of here," he told me. The possibility of getting away buoyed me. Dad understood this and believed boarding school would be a chance for me to expand my opportunities. He warned me of the dangers of becoming a small fish in a big pond, having no idea how sharply my fortunes at Kew-Forest had plummeted over the course of the last two years as I became more socially awkward and incapable of impressing my teachers.

"I know you need to push yourself and I think you need a new place to do it." It's the closest he came to admitting this had all become too much for me—his being at the House at the mercy of forces I couldn't possibly understand; my having to deal with my mother by myself since Fritz had gone to college; my living in a constant state of uncertainty as to when or whether I could count on either one of them to be there for me.

One evening, we were waiting in the library at the House for my grandfather to get back from the Brooklyn office so Dad could let him know I would most likely be going to boarding school. We had to discuss the tuition for the upcoming semester as well as my needing to withdraw from Kew-Forest. Dad seemed to be steeling himself in preparation for a conversation he dreaded.

My grandfather, of course, was against my going. He complained about what a waste of money it would be, insisting that Kew-Forest was a perfectly fine school, the best.

But Dad held his ground. When the time came, if the time came, the tuition would be paid. I didn't know until a very long time after this, but while my grandfather made a big show of bemoaning the cost of anything he disapproved of, he never put his hand in his pocket for anything. All of our expenses, from the rent we paid him to tuition for school and camp, came from trust funds he'd set up before we were even born. Dad acted like he didn't know that, either—and perhaps he didn't.

With only a week to go, Walker's called again to say they'd found a place for me after all: they'd solved the problem by putting an extra bed in a double room to turn it into a triple. I called Dad to let him know and promised to stop by the House the day before I left for Connecticut.

"Don't take this the wrong way," he said, "but I'm glad you're going."

So was I.

47

In my absence over the summer, my grandfather had turned the breakfast room at the House, a secondary dining room between the kitchen and the library, into newspaper-clipping central. As soon as Donald's Grand Hyatt project had gotten off the ground in the late 1970s, he started clipping articles from the two New York newspapers he had delivered every day: *The New York Times* and the *Daily News*. In the interim, he also subscribed to the *New York Post*, which seemed more favorable to Donald than the others.

Over the years, the only gift my mother gave my grandfather that he actually seemed to appreciate—other than a framed needlepoint embroidery of a Native American wearing a headdress— was a single-sheet cutter that made it easier to clip articles out of newspapers. Now he had several of them.

Donald had hired a clipping service, and whenever he came to the House, he brought my grandfather accordion folders full of interviews and profiles from other papers and magazines. Not only was three-quarters of the table now covered, but my grandfather put clippings on the shelves of the étagère by the bay window and on the seats of some of the dining chairs that he had pulled away from the table and lined up against the walls. There were only two chairs left unencumbered at the far end of the table, where, presumably, he and Gam had their meals.

Almost every time I went to the House, Donald and my grandfather stood there discussing the clippings, rearranging them.

One afternoon, Dad and I were in the library watching a Mets game. I was telling him about the sports facilities I'd seen on my tour of Walker's when Donald came in holding up a clipping and said, "Hey, Freddy. Remember this?"

Donald's smile was genuine enough to draw me and my father to get off the couch and walk over to him. Dad leaned in to take a closer look, then straightened up immediately. The headline of the *New York Post* article had the word "Steeplechase" in it. I would learn much later that Steeplechase Park, a much-loved Coney Island amusement park that was also the cornerstone of the local economy, had been the last project my father was involved in at Trump Management. It had also been an abject failure for my grandfather, one that had destroyed a Coney Island landmark and forcibly relocated hundreds of Black families, arguably ending his career as a developer. Trump Village, which had been completed three years before Steeplechase, was the last building project Fred ever completed. When it became clear that the obstacles in the way of Fred's making Steeplechase a success were probably insurmountable, he made Freddy the face of the debacle and saddled him with the blame.

The picture accompanying the 1966 article showed Freddy and another man crouching down with a tiger—an actual tiger—lying on the ground in front of them.

"Hey, honeybunch," Donald said to me. "Your dad was such a handsome guy, wasn't he?"

I might have agreed with him, but since the formerly "handsome guy" was standing right next to me, I didn't say anything. Dad looked at the floor. What struck me about the photograph—beyond the bizarre presence of the massive cat—was the expression on my father's face.

The man next to Dad was holding some papers right in front of the tiger's face. Dad had a pen, with which he was presumably going to sign the documents, but he was clearly calculating how to do that without having to get his hand too close to the tiger's

wide-open mouth. There's a self-consciousness in that calculation, as if he's aware he's supposed to look cool and unfazed but
can't quite pull it off. His lips are drawn in a tight line and his
entire body is tense. He can't help but look afraid. It's the only
picture I've ever seen in which he looks like me.

"Seems like forever ago," Dad said quietly.

"Really?" Donald laughed. "I remember it like it was yesterday." Which made no sense at all because at the time, Donald
was a nineteen-year-old college student in Philadelphia who had
no involvement in the Steeplechase project.

48

Freddy and Donald were mirror images of each other—one genuinely successful but cast as a failure, the other incapable of succeeding at anything but propped up by a father who evaluated his sons through a very different lens than any objective observer.

Fred thought Freddy's accomplishments and expertise as a pilot frivolous and beneath him, even though commercial aviation was considered the pinnacle of cool at the time my father was a sought-after professional. It was Donald's attitude, his disdain for the rules and other people, and his willingness to do anything to fit within his father's mold that appealed to Fred, that made him the recipient of tens of millions of dollars to maintain the illusion of a brilliance that never existed. In the wake of Donald's supposed great success at the Grand Hyatt, Fred had to give his middle son almost $4.7 million in the first eight months of 1979 just to keep him and his extravagant lifestyle afloat.

In the end, both sons were failures—Donald because he had none of the requisite skills to succeed on his own, and Freddy because he was made to be. My grandfather didn't hold Donald up because he was proud of him but because he knew Donald's "success" was his creation. By the same token, he deemed everything Freddy did—all of his interests, his hobbies, his passions, his choices of wife and friends—a personal affront. He considered his eldest son *his* failure, not just to be punished, but to be hidden away. It seemed at times that Fred felt a profound discomfort around Freddy, as if he sensed something about his namesake that he could neither accept nor acknowledge, something that repelled him.

For Donald, Fred's methodical dismantling of his older brother was a master class in how to identify and exploit other people's weaknesses, and eventually break them down. Donald was still a teenager when he began his apprenticeship, acting as his father's proxy to humiliate Freddy for daring to strike out on his own to fly 707s for TWA. Freddy had never considered Donald a rival—he was too young, too arrogant, too impulsive for that. But after a brief period of looking up to his older brother, Donald did consider Freddy a rival—until he no longer was.

It never occurred to anybody in my family that my grandfather didn't care about us, so we constructed a version of him in our heads that *did* care. Maryanne clung to the notion that there was still the possibility that her achievements in the legal profession would impress him; they didn't. Elizabeth literally clung to him when he passed through a room. Robert dutifully went to work in the dreary Avenue Z office of Trump Management to milk the "cash cow," even though it required nothing of him and would never garner him his father's notice or appreciation.

Nothing we did mattered, but that's a hard truth to take in, especially if you have dreams of accomplishing something. Those of us who were ambitious tried to convince ourselves that the only way to get noticed or be appreciated was to be the best at whatever it was we chose to do. But what we found out in the end was that, unless you were Donald, nothing—not getting straight As or flying professionally for TWA at the dawn of the jet age or becoming a federal court judge—was enough.

Fred didn't care about any of it. Despite the obvious favoritism he exhibited toward his middle son, in truth, he cared about Donald only to the extent that he could use him. He needed somebody with Donald's unselfconscious swagger, lack of self-reflection, and brazen ignorance of his inadequacies to be his avatar of success in a world beyond the unglamorous and provincial precincts of Brooklyn and Queens. Donald played his role to perfection. In a final bit of poetic justice, after decades of benefiting from his father's largesse and unconditional support, Donald would show how little he cared for his father (and how bad he actually was at business) by selling off his father's empire—the legacy my grandfather spent nearly eight decades creating—at a loss of several hundred million dollars.

But long before that, Donald and Maryanne made the cold calculation that helping Freddy would put them at odds with their father. They weren't simply co-opted in the project of destroying their brother; they were Fred's willing accomplices. They may once have had better instincts, but they had seen too much. Both of them had too much to lose by crossing Fred; and Donald in particular saw his potential fate—had *always* seen his potential fate—in Freddy's, whether he was aware of it or not.

Maryanne didn't bring my father back to the House after he was released from rehab in the summer of 1981 because she thought that was the best place for him to be or because she lacked the resources to help him independent of their father. She brought Freddy back to the House because that's where Fred wanted him.

There would be no more getting away, there would be no starting over, but *not* because my father had given up. He was still recuperating from his open-heart surgery but beginning to feel stronger, even hopeful. He still had ambition. In January 1979 Dad wrote, in neat all-caps print, a letter to the FAA on his Captain Fred C. Trump Jr. stationery:

Dear Sirs:

Enclosed please find my pilot certificate #145 2031—
    I would appreciate a new certificate, issued to me at my
current address:

    85-14 Midland Parkway
    Jamaica Estates, NY 11432

    Social Security Number = 126-30-1355
    Date of birth = 10/14/38
    Place of birth = Jamaica, New York

                                              Thanks,
                        (signed) Frederick Crist Trump
    Enc. Valid Certificate (to be replaced)
    Check to F.A.A. $200

But my grandfather had no intention of letting him go.

As far as Fred was concerned, his oldest son and his greatest
shame had brought his fate down on himself. Over the next
two years, my father withered under my grandfather's contempt,
relegated to his suffocating childhood bedroom and a maintenance crew on one of his father's properties—the same property
that was meant to launch Freddy's real estate career more than
a decade earlier.

Finally, it was no longer enough for Fred to keep Freddy financially dependent or to cut him out of any meaningful role in
the family—let alone the family business. Hiding him away—in
a Trump Village maintenance crew, in the House—and restrict-
ing his movements was a way to keep the wider world from
finding out about his own embarrassment and failure. In the be-

ginning of my father's dismantling, Fred seemed to enjoy wielding the complete power of the torturer.

When my father ultimately conceded my grandfather was right, that *he* was the problem, my grandfather came to the conclusion that having total control over a defeated human being, humiliating a person who no longer reacted to the humiliation, just wasn't fun anymore.

In mid-September 1981, I went to the House to say goodbye to my father before I left for boarding school. When I arrived, the back door was locked, so I rang the bell. I could hear the sound of the radio coming from my father's open bedroom window above me.

When no one came to the door, I rang again. I was beginning to think nobody was home. Finally, my grandmother, wearing an apron, opened the door. She stood in the doorway instead of letting me in.

I told her I'd come to say goodbye.

She told me my father wasn't home. I hesitated. It's not that I thought she was lying—I didn't. By then I'd been disappointed by my father enough to think the worst, to believe that he was perfectly capable of forgetting I was coming to see him even though I was leaving the next day and wouldn't be home for months. But I could tell there was something wrong. If Dad wasn't there, I could have waited for him or left him a note, but something about the way Gam blocked the door with her entire body made it clear that she didn't want me to come inside.

After an awkward hug, I got on my bike and rode the long way home. As I sped through the familiar side streets, my unease dissipated. Jamaica looked beautiful in the fading afternoon light. I couldn't wait to leave.

The beginning of the semester at Walker's passed in a blur. I remember spending a lot of time marveling at how difficult it was to be new—something I hadn't experienced since I was six years old, when everyone else starting at camp or Kew-Forest was new, too. I'd learned that it was unusual, and ill-advised, to start boarding school as a junior. Both of my roommates were new juniors, too, which might have helped, but they had a lot in common with each other and bonded quickly. They didn't leave me out, and we all got along; I just didn't fit in with them.

I tried out for the soccer team, read through my syllabi, bought my books and school supplies. I was surprised by how much independence we had. Despite being in the middle of nowhere and having no real amenities off campus other than a small group of stores a couple of miles down the road, including a McDonald's and the drugstore where everybody bought their cartons of cigarettes, we were left to our own devices when we weren't in class. Small groups pulled all-nighters in the lounge downstairs or in each other's rooms. Students could smoke in a room in the basement called the Fish Bowl or in designated areas outside, pretty much whenever they wanted. We had the run of the dining room long after meals were over.

And then, at ten o'clock on a Saturday night a couple of weeks in, Dunn, a PE teacher at Walker's whom I'd known since the early 1970s because she was also a counselor at camp, walked up to me in the auditorium where we'd been watching a movie, a piece of scrap paper in her hand. She told me she needed to tell me something, and as we walked out, she relayed the message: call your mother, or your grandparents if she isn't home.

When I got back to my dorm, I made a collect call to my mother from the pay phone in the stairwell right next to my room. When she didn't answer, I called the House. My grandfather picked up, sounding the same as ever. Although he conceded that my father was sick enough to be admitted to the hospital, he told me it was nothing to worry about. "Call your mother in the morning," he said. It was only when I pressed him that he acknowledged my father's situation was serious. *Yes, it's his heart. Yes, I'd say it's serious.* But he spoke with no sense of urgency at all. He told me again to go to sleep and call my mother in the morning. She'd fill me in.

I called her again immediately after hanging up, and this time she answered—she'd been on her way back home from the House when I called the first time—and she was crying. My father was dead.

I don't know how long I sat on the floor of the stairwell with the phone receiver hanging on its cord next to me. Eventually, Kate, the dorm proctor who had the room next to mine, came to check on me. She put the phone to her ear and hung it up. "Are you OK?"

I looked at her but didn't say anything.

Only half an hour earlier, I'd been talking and laughing with people who might become my friends. I thought maybe I would belong there someday.

I learned later that an ambulance had been called in the afternoon. My grandfather called his other four children to tell them my father had been taken to the emergency room, but he reached only Donald and Elizabeth, who drove out to Queens to join their parents. Donald called my mother to let her know Dad was in bad shape, and she drove immediately to the House even though my father had been taken to Queens General Hospital only five minutes from our building. Then he and Elizabeth went to the movies. It didn't seem to occur to anyone that they should be with my father.

It was just before 9:30 P.M. when Donald and Elizabeth returned (they probably saw *Arthur*; they probably ate popcorn). The hospital had just called my grandfather with the news that my father was dead. Donald left to drive back to the city, and Elizabeth, after making a cup of tea, went upstairs to her room without saying a word.

My grandmother followed Elizabeth upstairs and my mother stayed in the library with my grandfather to discuss how my brother and I should get home. At first, my grandfather insisted it wasn't necessary for Fritz, who was at college in Orlando, to return home at all. My mother told him her cousin Van lived near the campus and he could make the arrangements and take Fritz to the airport. Walker's was only a two-hour-and-forty-five-minute drive from New York, so they agreed I should take a bus in the morning.

My mother called Van first; she wanted to make sure somebody was with Fritz when she broke the news. Van drove to the dorm and brought my brother back to their house to spend the night. Then she called my house parents to tell them what had happened, and they gave Dunn the message for me to call home.

As soon as I got back to my room, Dunn told me I'd be staying with her that night. I packed my bags, and told Dunn and my roommates that I didn't want anybody else to know what had happened. I was adamant about this. I felt it would make it impossible for me to be myself if everybody knew, as if the news of my father's death would taint me somehow.

We walked to the dorm where Dunn was a house parent. A

few students were waiting outside of her apartment. I didn't look at them and stepped inside as soon as Dunn opened the door.

Dunn and I spread a couple of sheets and a blanket on the floor and she threw me a couple of pillows. People started knocking on the door. By eleven, a steady stream of students came by to tell me how sorry they were, to see how I was doing, to gawk. I hadn't even met most of them and barely recognized the rest. I felt very speeded up; everything was brighter than it should have been. I sat on the floor, leaning against the couch with a blanket around my shoulders, wondering aloud why it was so cold.

Eventually, they all left, but I couldn't sleep. I spent the night shivering, and by the time the sun rose, I was numb with exhaustion. After Dunn woke up, she offered to make breakfast, but I wasn't hungry. She got ready and drove me to the bus station in Hartford.

I fell asleep as soon as I took my seat, and I didn't wake up until the bus pulled into a bay at the Port Authority Bus Terminal in Manhattan. My vision was blurry from exhaustion and the fluorescent lights glared as I walked through the terminal, my bag slung over my shoulder, trying to find the right exit. I hadn't been to Port Authority in years, and I was so tired—more tired than I'd been before I slept—that it took me a while to orient myself. I finally found the sign for the Forty-Second Street exit. When I got outside, I saw my mother's car idling at the curb halfway down the block.

My mother had already picked my brother up from the airport and he was in the passenger seat, so I slid into the back. We all said hi. Mom asked me how the trip had been. I shrugged.

One of my best friends from Kew-Forest was waiting for me in the lobby when we got back to the Highlander. Upstairs, I grabbed a couple of Pepsis out of the refrigerator and she and I went to my room. After I stood awkwardly for a few minutes— I rambled about Walker's, about what a weird experience it had been so far, how different the people were—she finally told me to sit down.

I leaned against the wall, a couple of pillows propped behind me. She put Billy Joel's *Streetlife Serenade* on the turntable, then sat at the end of the bed facing me, legs crossed. We talked a bit—about Kew-Forest and our friends—but mostly we listened to the music, which we'd heard hundreds of times before. She stayed with me as the sky darkened. Without meaning to, I fell asleep.

When I woke up, I was alone. The merest sliver of a crescent moon hung outside my window.

51

I was getting ready for the funeral two days later when I realized I'd forgotten to bring my hair dryer from school. I asked Fritz if I could use his. The plastic covering the heating coils was missing and a strand of my hair got caught in the fan. My hair started to burn. The smell was awful. I thought of my father's impending cremation. For some reason I thought that was funny, but when I looked in the mirror, I was grimacing.

After visiting the cemetery where my father's ashes were going to be buried in the family plot, we went back to the House. Nobody outside of the immediate family was there, no food had been prepared, and nobody had anything to say.

After an impersonal ceremony at the crematorium, I had tried once again to convince my grandfather not to bury my father's ashes. Dad was so adamant about it that I'd known since I was eight that this wasn't what he wanted. I came as close as I ever had to raising my voice to him, and he came as close as he ever had to showing his anger. I tried to explain to him how wrong it was, how profoundly disturbing it would be for Dad to be trapped in that earth. But my grandfather wasn't listening, and I lost the argument.

I couldn't stay in the library with the rest of them, but none of my old haunts appealed to me. I didn't want to be there at all.

I climbed the back stairs to the second floor. The door to Liz's room was slightly ajar, but I knew she was in there. I took a few steps farther down the hall to the Cell, but when I saw the stripped mattress and a couple of his white button-down shirts on wire hangers in an otherwise empty closet, I doubled back to the stairs leading to the attic. I was surprised to see the cot where Dad had slept for a few months after he and my mother split up, still covered with his old army blanket. The black-and-white TV was on the floor next to an old manual typewriter. I walked over, picked up the blanket, and sat down. I rested my face in it.

It smelled dark, and sharp, and like my father.

52

The day after the funeral, my mother and brother drove me back to Walker's. I'd been gone for three days. A few minutes after we reached the more rural roads outside Hartford, Fritz pulled over and let me drive. It was a beautiful day and the sunlight streamed through the leaves, just starting to turn. Whenever the road narrowed or a car passed me, I tensed up. My brother, now in the passenger seat next to me, peeled my tightly clenched fingers one by one from the steering wheel and then gently put them back. "The trick is to relax," he said. I remembered sitting on my father's lap behind the steering wheel on the way out to Montauk. This was harder.

Once I got back to school, I took up the habits of smoking and sarcasm. There was no support system, so I tried to create my own, which was easier when I cloaked my despair in dark humor and asked somebody if I could have a light. The regular smokers in the Fish Bowl formed a loose-knit community. The first time I bummed a Benson & Hedges Deluxe Ultra Light 100 from a sophomore I was friendly with, I became part of the group. It helped that as soon as I took that first drag, my entire body relaxed. I'd had no idea how tightly wound I'd been, and I almost fainted when the tension left my body.

Academically, I was able to keep up at first. English and American history kept me especially engaged, not only because they'd always been my best subjects and the teachers were incredibly demanding, but because the reading took me out of myself. At the beginning of the semester, I'd learned that Mrs. Shea, the history teacher, had a reputation for being very serious about her subject; she was so exacting a taskmaster that students in her class rarely got any grade higher than a B. This gave me something to strive for.

The work was so intense, and the workload so potentially overwhelming, that she had advised us to find somebody to study with. I didn't know anybody well enough to ask, but Parker, a kid who lived in my dorm on the floor above mine, asked if I wanted to partner with her. When I got back from New York, we picked up where we left off. It helped to have somebody to keep me focused. We worked hard. She called me "Sexy," a familiarity I found both comforting and confusing.

53

I checked in with my mother once a week and spoke to my brother two or three times, but I always felt worse afterward. I couldn't articulate what I was feeling. None of us had ever had the language to talk about our family's dysfunction—we'd never wanted to talk about it; it was too scary. Neither of them could help me, although they made it clear that they were suffering, too.

I believed my brother, but I couldn't understand what my mother was going through. She and my father had been divorced for eleven years and apart for almost fourteen. After they split up, almost every interaction she had with my father ended with her railing against him—how incompetent he was, how irresponsible, what a terrible father; how much she hated him.

Right after she told me he was dead, she added that she really had loved him once. I couldn't process this totally incongruous information, and it left me feeling bereft.

After every conversation I had with them, a darkness lurked; it grew, and it began to take over. A feeling of guilt began to creep up on me. When I told Fritz about it, he said, "You *should* feel guilty," but he didn't explain why, and I just had to take his word for it.

I didn't speak to him again until we were both home for Thanksgiving. I was angry, because I knew he was right. My father was dead and I didn't even miss him. Most of the time, I doubted if I'd loved him. Without question, I hadn't loved him enough.

In the three days I'd been home for the wake and funeral, each one of my aunts and uncles had approached me with terse versions of a man I didn't recognize, as if awkwardly bestowing a gift: "Like wealthy men who care not how they give."

The words Donald and my grandfather had always used to describe my father—kind, generous, sensitive, trusting—were meant to be insults, euphemisms for "weak." "Such a great guy. So handsome," Donald said now, because he didn't have anything else to say. And then he winked.

"What a guy, honeybunch," Robert offered. "What a sweet, funny guy."

Elizabeth didn't say anything at all.

Maryanne came over to me, but she didn't hug me or even shake my hand. It seemed to cost her, but she finally said, "Your dad was the best of us."

But how, when they made it impossible for him to be any of those things? Why couldn't he be any of those things for me?

None of them called me after I got back to school, so I had no frame of reference within which to understand this new information. To me, it was revisionist history. I only knew the man they humiliated and ridiculed until he could no longer fight back. They took my father away from me before I was even born. By the time I was old enough to be aware, he was so steeped in self-loathing, so ravaged by drinking and chain-smoking, he bore absolutely no resemblance to the portrait they sketched. I didn't have the first idea how to grapple with any of it.

It would've been terrible if I'd loved my father as deeply as I should have, if he and I had had a great relationship, but it was so much worse because my grandfather created the conditions that made those things impossible. By the time Fred decided he no longer wanted to bear the burden of being constantly reminded of his greatest failure—he had given this weak, unmanly creature his name, after all—he'd already conditioned the rest of us not to care.

When my father became ill enough to be confined to his bed, my grandfather took the opportunity to deprive him of alcohol, without regard for the consequence. In addition to being sick, then, Freddy suffered from severe alcohol withdrawal, which would've stressed his heart and made him that much sicker, that much easier to ignore.

When it was over, Fred was finally able to proceed as if his oldest son, and, by extension, Freddy's children, had never existed. Fritz and I were still required to meet certain obligations, but without our knowing it, our grandfather had already erased us on paper, even though a couple of decades would pass before we found that out.

My father's tragedy was that ultimately, he believed every lie his father told about him. My tragedy was that I did, too.

54

On the floor of the closet where my mother kept the basket with our birth certificates and other documents, there was a box of old photographs. The morning my mother and Fritz drove me back to Walker's, I sifted through it surreptitiously and took a framed five-by-seven. I hid it in my bag underneath my clothes.

Back at school, I put the picture on the desk at the end of my bed. It had been taken in late 1965, when I was only a few months old. Dad and Mom sit next to each other on our living room couch, the quintessential 1960s couple—her bleached-blond hair cut in a bob and held in place with a tortoiseshell headband; his brown hair parted on the side, slicked back. My mother, wearing a black-and-white off-the-shoulder dress and a string of pearls, looks straight at the camera, her lips curled in a carefully modulated smile. She cradles me in her right arm.

Fritz sits on Dad's lap, also looking straight at the camera, Dad's arms around him.

I'm looking up at Dad, a serious, slightly grumpy expression on my face. And Dad is looking down at me—smiling as if he and I were the whole world.

I became obsessed with that picture. When I was alone in my room, I spent too much time looking at it, as if it contained some secret I could unlock if only I looked hard enough. Sometimes at night when I couldn't sleep, I brought the picture to bed and studied it by the light of the streetlamp that streamed through the window.

The picture haunted me. Nothing about it seemed real except the way my father smiled at me.

55

I was getting less and less sleep, which made it harder for me to focus. My play on the soccer field—the one thing that I should have been able to count on—was deteriorating, and worse, I didn't enjoy being on the team. Concentrating in class was becoming almost impossible. I could barely keep up with subjects like French and math. I fell behind and my grades began to slide.

Then I started having the nightmare.

> I stand in the middle of a clearing surrounded by maple and ash trees in full bloom, looking for my father's tombstone by the light of the full moon. When I find it, I trace his name, carved deep into the marble, with my fingers.

And then I woke up. That was it. Even though nothing happened, there was something sinister lurking there, and I dreaded having the dream again.

I tried to put off sleep as long as I could. I stayed in the library until they kicked me out. I hung out in the Fish Bowl or the lounge until everybody else had gone to bed. Eventually, I had no choice but to go back to my room.

> I kneel on my father's grave, digging through the sod with my bare hands. I feel a sense of urgency as I dig past rocks and tree roots until my knuckles bleed and my fingernails tear.

Every night in my dream the digging became more frantic and the urgency greater.

Finally, I have made it through all six feet of the dark
pungent dirt and reached the metal box that holds my
father's ashes. I want to open it, to set him free, but fear and
uncertainty hold me back at first. Suddenly I realize this is
a bad idea. I never should have come to this place. But I am
compelled to continue. I wait, catch my breath, and at last I
open the box.

My father's disembodied head, green and swollen, lies
inside. His eyes, still open, stare blankly. I drop the box and
try to climb back up, but I can't find any purchase and—

I sat bolt upright. I thought I screamed, but when I looked
over at my roommates, they slept, undisturbed. I couldn't get
my heart rate to slow down. I swung my legs over the side of
the bed. I grabbed my chest and tried to steady my breathing. I
tried not to scream again.

56

I had just gotten out of the shower when a sophomore who lived down the hall told me all the juniors needed to meet at the gym. She didn't know why, but she said it was important and I needed to leave right away. I was annoyed and almost didn't go. There was a chill in the air and my hair was still wet. I had a lot of homework. But I didn't want to risk getting in trouble, so I got dressed quickly and made my way to the gym. On the way, I saw a van that looked like an ambulance parked near the front entrance to my dorm.

Other juniors were gathered at the entrance to the gym. A senior told us to go downstairs, and then another directed some of us to the locker room and the rest to the equipment room down the hall. A few other kids from my class were already there. Nobody seemed to know what was going on, and after a few minutes of idle speculation, we got quiet. There was a tension in the room, and I thought about the ambulance I'd seen. Maybe something was going on, something bad, and they were keeping us here until they'd gotten the situation under control or, worse, until they could figure out how to break the bad news to us about whatever terrible thing had happened.

My heart started pounding and I felt short of breath.

By the time the door opened, I was having a hard time staying in my seat. I was braced for something awful. A few seniors filed in and lined up in front of the door. What the fuck was happening?

They looked so serious.

Every muscle in my body was tensed almost past endurance. I was ready to run.

One of them droned on about something. It seemed clear something was wrong. And then she said, "Trump! Come up here."

I gripped the seat of my chair with both hands. I couldn't move.

I recognized one of the seniors from the night I stayed at Dunn's apartment. She came over to where I was sitting, but before she could say a word, I started to sob.

"Whoa, it's OK. We just wanted to give you this." She wrapped an old varsity jacket around my shoulders. I couldn't stop crying. She tried to calm me down, but I could tell I was freaking her out.

I had completely ruined an old school tradition in which seniors handed down artifacts with some symbolic importance to juniors, but it went completely over my head. I felt so stupid and so relieved. The pent-up terror began to leave my body. I hugged the jacket tightly around me, not because I knew what it meant, or even cared, but because I felt so alone and without comfort and thought I might unravel.

I bent over and covered my face with my hands and kept sobbing.

Everybody stared at me. Nobody knew what to do.

I skipped dinner and went straight to my room. I sat alone at my desk looking at the picture. Rage surged through me. It was bad enough that I was constantly exhausted, that I couldn't think straight, that I couldn't keep up with my classes or play soccer. Now everybody thought I was a fucking basket case. Crying in front of them was embarrassing, but having no control over myself filled me with shame. And what were they even thinking, anyway? What a stupid waste of my time. And now everybody would know I was a fucking mess, a loser who couldn't keep it together.

I picked up the picture. I hated how it mocked me with its

perfection. I looked at my father's face—he was tan and looked genuinely happy, but I knew it was all bullshit. Images from my dream intruded—the grave, my bloody hands, my father's severed head, and, worst of all, the look of anguish frozen on his face.

I resented being so diminished. I resented him. I resented my mother. I resented my brother. I resented the fucking idiots who gave me the jacket. I couldn't remember the last time I'd felt love or joy or peace. I didn't think I ever would again. All I had was anger, and there was nothing to defuse it, so I stoked it.

I stood up and slammed the picture against a corner of my desk as hard as I could. The wood frame splintered, and shattered glass flew everywhere. I ran out of the room, slamming the door shut. I flew down the stairs and out the side door; I sprinted toward the road that bordered the north side of the campus. It was dark and quiet as I ran past an abandoned field and isolated houses and empty lots until there was nothing but a dense stand of trees on either side of the road.

I had no idea how far from school I was. I didn't care.

It was late when I got back to the dorm. I didn't want to see my roommates, so instead of going to my room, I climbed another flight of stairs and went to see Parker. I couldn't think what else to do, and she was the closest thing I had to a friend.

Her door was open, and when she saw me, she said, "Hey! Where've you been?" My roommates had alerted the house parents after finding the broken glass on the floor. People had been looking for me ever since. I assumed I was in trouble, but instead of going to turn myself in, I sat down.

"Seriously, where did you go?" Parker asked.

"Just down the road. I needed to get out of here."

"I have to let Mrs. Pierce know you're back, OK?" Parker was a dorm proctor, so she had her own responsibilities to deal with. "I'll be right back. Don't go anywhere."

I nodded.

"Promise me," she said.

"I promise." I tried not to sound sarcastic.

As I waited, I noticed there was blood on my right hand from a pretty deep gash near the knuckle of my index finger. I'd probably gotten it from the glass but couldn't remember. As soon as I saw it, I felt it sting. I made a fist and it started bleeding again. Before Parker and Mrs. Pierce got back, I wrapped a Kleenex around the cut and shoved my hand into my pocket. I didn't want them to think I'd done it on purpose.

"We've been worried about you," Mrs. Pierce said. "Are you OK?"

"Yeah, I'm fine."

"I think we need to call your mom," she said. "Can you come with me?" It was a rhetorical question, but I said no. I refused to sit there while she talked to my mother (and probably the dean of students) about me in the third person.

She hesitated, as if debating whether to press the point. I crossed my legs. "OK. Wait here then." She gave Parker a meaningful look, then left to make her calls.

I stretched out my legs and leaned my head against the wall. I felt wired but also empty and blissfully detached from everything.

"I guess that's it," I said to Parker.

"We'll see," she said.

They decided to send me home the next day. This time, my mother picked me up.

57

I mostly stayed in my bedroom during the month I was home. My mother was in a grim mood, and I was better off reading, chipping away at my school assignments, and writing letters. I spoke to my Kew-Forest friends on the phone but didn't see them very often; it was hard for me to be around people because I thought I had to pretend that everything was fine and didn't know how to explain all the ways it wasn't.

Twice a week, I had therapy with Dr. Rice. I don't know if I would have been able to open up to anybody, but, given our history, there was no way I was going to open up to him. He was in his sixties by then, conservative and cold. I was grateful he never pulled the human anatomy textbook off the shelf, but I had no intention of sharing my feelings with this straitlaced stranger who seemed devoid of empathy.

At the end of one session, he pulled out his calendar and asked about future appointments.

"I'll be away for a week over Thanksgiving, so let's look at the following week," he said.

"I thought next week was our last session," I said.

"I think that would be a mistake," he said. "We need to discuss alternatives to your going back to boarding school anytime soon."

"What do you mean by alternatives?" I felt a chill run down my spine.

"There are a few possibilities that we should seriously consider."

I hated the fact that he kept saying "we," as if "we" were in

anything together, or as if *he* had any say over what happened
in my life.

"I believe you should take the rest of the school year off. You
can start up again at Walker's next September, start your junior
year over with a clean slate. Returning to Kew-Forest in January
is also a possibility."

I was so panicked by the thought of being held back—of having to stay home—that I didn't hear anything else he said. Leaving
boarding school, even if it were to go back to Kew-Forest, would
have felt like a catastrophic failure.

I needed to prove that I controlled my future, that I knew
what was best for me.

I showed up to the next appointment the following week.
And I lied.

My brother came home from college with a beard and an earring, wearing a bandanna like a kerchief on his head. He felt like
a stranger, and we avoided each other. I wanted to stay home
by myself instead of going to the House for Thanksgiving, but I
was told that wasn't an option.

My grandfather, Donald, and Ivana, who was eight months
pregnant, were as cheerful and voluble as ever, but the rest of
them had the presence of mind to be more subdued. My grandmother barely spoke; she looked sunken and grey, but she managed to prepare the Thanksgiving meal.

I wore pants and a baggy sweater instead of the usual skirt or
dress I wore for formal family occasions. Fritz had taken off the
bandanna, but the earring did not go over well. My grandfather
looked at us both with disdain. For the first time in memory, he
didn't offer to buy my hair.

After we filled our plates and took our places at the table, somebody said, "The prayer?" They bowed their heads. I felt such contempt for them as they recited:

Come Lord Jesus
Be our guest.
Bless this meal
Which thou hast given us.
Amen

Then Maryanne said, "A toast." We raised our glasses of apple juice and Coke, which is all that was ever offered. "To Freddy," she said.

My grandmother sat next to me, and I could see her lips trembling.

"To Freddy," the rest of us repeated.

Except for my grandfather; he didn't bother.

58

After my last session with Dr. Rice, I told my mother I planned to go back to Walker's the day after Thanksgiving. I knew the price of being allowed to stay there was to pretend I was OK, which meant I only had to keep it together for the three weeks between Thanksgiving and Christmas. At that point, I'd have another two weeks to regroup before spring semester.

When I returned to campus, teachers made allowances; students gave me a wide berth. I tried out for the basketball team and made varsity, I dug in to English and history, I continued to suck at French and math and chemistry. But I could do three weeks.

By Christmas, the family had decided enough time had passed. There were no toasts, no concessions to Dad's absence. Donald and Ivana had a baby in tow in addition to their toddler, Donny, which made it easier for me to slip away. I went down to the basement. I didn't want to turn the overhead fluorescent light on, so I fumbled around in the dark trying to find the switch that turned the bar lights on. After I found it, I sat on a barstool and opened my well-worn copy of *The Martian Chronicles*.

When we got back to the Highlander that afternoon, my mother told us she had one more present for each of us. They were, she said, from Dad. The hairs on the back of my neck stood up until she explained what she meant. After my grandfather closed my father's checking account, he gave the money to my mother to give to us. She had used the proceeds to get us Christmas presents—from Dad.

She handed me a velvet jewelry box. Inside was an emerald

ring. Emerald was my birthstone, and the ring itself was beautiful, a classic emerald cut set in a yellow gold band. I didn't wear
it often—I was afraid I would knock it against something and
lose the stone—but I brought it with me wherever I went. Years
later, I had the jewel appraised. It was glass.

By the time the second semester of junior year began, I felt more
rested, less anxious. I still had trouble falling asleep; I still had
nightmares, but they were different, less threatening.

I played basketball, and I tried out for the part of Sandy in
The Prime of Miss Jean Brodie. I didn't get cast, but the director
made me the understudy. It didn't really end up meaning anything, but it made me part of the cast. I filled in at a couple of
rehearsals and helped out the crew. I had tutors to help me catch
up with math and French. I had to improve my grades as quickly
as possible for the sake of college applications. I still worked my
ass off in American history, but it was English that got most of
my effort and attention.

My teacher, Mrs. Nelson, looked like she'd stepped out of
the frame of a 1950s TV show—the only thing missing was an
apron—but she didn't suffer fools. Her course, more than any
I'd taken before, had a profound impact on how I approached
reading and writing.

Her reading list was eclectic and idiosyncratic and covered
every genre. She assigned Archibald MacLeish's *J.B.* and Eugene
O'Neill's *Long Day's Journey into Night*; the poems of Edna St.
Vincent Millay and Edith Wharton's *Ethan Frome*; but it was
William Faulkner's *The Sound and the Fury* that changed my life.

Mrs. Nelson's English class saved me that year, not only because of the reading, but because she took me seriously. She was
not a warm and fuzzy person, but I felt more supported by her

than by anybody else, even though we never discussed anything beyond the work.

Spring brought possibilities. The air was thin and the April light spread through it, bright and sharp, with a clarity I hadn't felt in a long time. As I walked from one building to the next on my way to classes or the gym or my room, music blared from open dorm windows—songs from *The Who by Numbers*, *CSN*, *Chariots of Fire*, *Pretenders II*, *Beauty and the Beat*, Soft Cell's *Non-Stop Erotic Cabaret*, a weird mélange of classic rock and whatever was in the Top 40—and it was easier out in the open to feel like I belonged, even if the feeling was illusory.

I made friends, but for the first time in my life, it took effort. I was altered, I knew I was altered, a feeling that pervaded everything I did and rendered me self-conscious. But I didn't know how to find the way back to myself. Suddenly, nothing came easily. I became insecure, which made me try too hard; I walked around wounded and often felt misunderstood. I became the kind of person other people mocked and talked about behind her back.

The only place I had left was camp.

59

I told myself that as soon as I set foot on camp property that summer for my final year in the Junior Counselor Training Program, all of the trauma of the last nine months would fall away and I would be magically restored. The illusion lasted until my friends came up to me to say how sorry they were about my father. Because I wanted it to stop—I was not going to have my summer defined in that way—I shrugged it off. "That's OK. He was a drunk." His death set me apart when I most needed to belong, and every time somebody mentioned it I was reminded that I no longer did.

From the time I was six or seven, I looked up to the JCs. Set apart from the rest of us by their all-white uniforms, they were what I aspired to be. The JC unit song was an anthem of their strength, their dedication, and their attitude.

Every summer since I became a JC I, my schedule had become more regimented, and the focus had shifted from learning to achievement and responsibility. This suited me perfectly, and having made it all the way to be an assistant counselor felt like a tremendous achievement. At that point, the only real difference between us and full counselors was the fact that we didn't get paid.

Since I had been the only JC III in the entire camp the previous summer, I expected to be the only JC IV this year. Instead, there were now two of us. Joan Henry, whom I barely knew, had started at the camp only the summer before, which meant while I was done with almost all of my requirements in sailing, archery, riflery, swimming, and land sports, Joan was starting from scratch. Even though we were the same age, I didn't consider us peers, but she was able to participate in the program because the brass had drastically modified the requirements for her.

The lack of ACs meant the camp didn't have enough coverage. Instead of living with the junior counselors during the half of the summer we worked at the day camp, as we normally would have done, we spent the entire summer in the unit we'd been assigned to as counselors while we worked at the day camp, effectively doubling the normal workload, eliminating most of our downtime, and making it almost impossible to spend time with the other JCs.

I was still allowed to participate in sailing races on the weekends, but I rarely got to shoot archery. When I got a chance to practice one day, shooting left-handed just to challenge myself, Judy, the JC head counselor, pulled me aside to remind me that I was an assistant counselor. "You need to focus on your unit and your campers." I'd been spending the bulk of whatever free time I had with my friends over at the JC unit, but she said that needed to stop as well.

As the summer ground on, they kept putting limits on me. I tried, and mostly failed, to focus on the work of being a counselor, but the truth was, I just wanted to be a camper again.

60

O n the last night of the summer, the entire camp, dressed in our uniforms, gathered at the outdoor theater for Cup Night. Each unit presented its awards for their Best Camper and Sportsmanship, but it was an especially important night for the junior counselors: if we had met all of our requirements, we received our major pins and the certificates representing that we'd completed our years. If we returned, we would be full counselors.

When the time came at the end of the evening, all the JCs formed a receiving line up the hill to the side of the benches. When a JC's name was announced, she ran down to the stage to receive her year certificate, an acknowledgment that she had successfully completed her training, and then hugged each counselor on her way back up the hill.

After I got my year, I went through the same process until I reached Becca, one of my counselors whom I'd known since my first year at camp who was also my best friend, even though she was three years older than I was. It looked like she'd been crying. I assumed she was sad because it was our last night, so I smiled and told her to cheer up. I felt light and happy for the first time in a long time, even knowing we would all be inconsolable when it was time to leave for home the next day.

Finally, the time came for the most important award: the Service Cup, the camp's highest honor awarded to an assistant counselor. Judy was standing with an envelope in her hand. I felt a thrill of excitement.

There was only me and Joan, and I was the only one who could possibly qualify. It's not simply that I'd been at camp ten years longer, but I had achieved at the highest level for that entire decade. From the time I was six, my evaluations had included words and phrases like "mature," "responsible," "enthusiastic," "an ideal camper," "a joy to have around," "a great achiever," "a leading force," "a true asset to the program," "the perfect camper." As I'd progressed through the program, I believed it was my job to live up to expectations, which meant not simply playing by the rules but excelling.

As Judy took the piece of paper out of the envelope, it got very quiet. I slowed my breathing, my hands gripping my knees.

"The winner of tonight's Service Cup," she announced, "is Joan Henry."

At first there was total silence. It probably lasted for only a beat, but in my memory, it stretched out for a painful interval. "Oh, my God," I said. Finally, the spell broke; the applause started. I don't remember anything else.

Becca told me later that, in the voting for the Service Cup, I'd received unanimous support from the JCs and the counselors. But the brass—the unit heads, the camp directors—had overruled them. Becca, who had always been close with certain members of the brass in ways I never was, met with Berry, the owner of the camp, a couple of days before Cup Night, to lobby her on my behalf. Berry was annoyed at having her decision questioned.

"This is not a lifetime achievement award," she said, contradicting the universally held belief among campers, counselors, and JCs that it was, indeed, a lifetime achievement award—or, at least, meant to honor work over the four years in the program. "The Service Cup is for work done over the course of one summer. And Mary did not have a good summer."

In the end, it was camp—the place that had saved my life, the place where I had worked the hardest to make a case for myself—that finally answered the question my mother had been posing to me since the first time she put me in bed next to her to suffocate through the night: Did I matter?

And the answer was no.

PART IV

The Only Way Out Is Through

I have been a stranger here in my own land: all
my life.

—SOPHOCLES, *Antigone*

61

2017–Present

I flew out of my shoe. When I looked behind me, my far-too-expensive three-inch heel was jammed between two cobblestones a few feet from the entrance to the East Wing of the White House. I hopped back to retrieve it and stood on one foot while I slipped it back on. As soon as I took my first step, I knew I was in trouble. The heel had been knocked off-center just enough to make me feel like I was walking at a slant.

Off-balance and out of control was a perfect description for how I felt about spending the evening with my estranged family at the White House on this April night in 2017. As a practical matter, however, it was less than ideal. Our destination was the Oval Office, which, even with properly working shoes, was a good distance across gleaming (and slippery) marble floors.

Our group comprised my aunt Maryanne, my brother, and my sister-in-law, the only members of my family I'd seen consistently in the eight years since Ivanka's wedding, as well as my aunt Elizabeth, uncle Rob, cousins, spouses, and my aunts' friends. We were waiting outside the Oval Office for Donald to finish his meeting with congressional leaders when I felt my heel give way.

"Help me!" I yelled. The only thing that could be worse than screaming in the Rose Garden would have been falling *into* the Rose Garden. Luckily, one of Maryanne's friends grabbed my arm and pulled me back before I landed in the shrubbery. I thanked my rescuer and thought, Jesus Christ, everybody is going to think I'm drunk. I took a deep breath and reminded myself that none of this mattered—it would all be over soon.

After the meeting broke, our group joined Donald for pictures in the Oval Office and then made our way upstairs to the residence. By the time I got to the second floor, I felt the beginnings of a headache.

I regretted my decision to attend the birthday party for my aunts Maryanne and Elizabeth almost as soon as I accepted the invitation. I'd been in a deep depression since the early-morning hours of November 9, 2016—Election Night—and since then, my sense of despair had only worsened. At the time, I lived in a mostly Republican town, and although politics had never interfered with my friendships before, Donald's ascension to the White House had ended most of them, leaving me feeling increasingly isolated and self-conscious.

I knew Donald, empowered in a way that was unthinkable, would be destructive; I knew he would commit atrocities, but I existed in a limbo of uncertainty and dread during the seventy-three-day interregnum, trying my best not to imagine what they might be. My only hope was that there would be constraints placed upon him, that the system would hold.

A week after he took office, I was sitting on the couch in my living room, doom-scrolling through Twitter with MSNBC on in the background, when the news about Donald's Muslim ban broke. I jumped to my feet and paced around the room as the chaos unfolded and the details, as muddled as they were at first, made clear just how far-reaching and depraved the ban was meant to be, thanks to its chief architect, the unspeakably vile Stephen Miller. The contours of the horrors Donald and his chosen deputies planned to inflict on us started to come into focus less than a week after the inauguration.

I was staring at the TV in disbelief from my position in the middle of the room when my daughter, a sophomore in high school, came through the front door. I didn't ask her how school was; I didn't ask if she wanted a snack or if she had any homework.

I said, "Av, do you understand what's going on?" My voice was raised, and she took a step back. "This is fascism." I gestured at the television and she looked at me like I'd lost my mind. "He's a fascist."

That's when I recognized the extent to which my fate had become intertwined with Donald's. Beyond the election itself, that was the first chink in the armor of American democracy (to the extent it existed), which wasn't nearly as strong as many of us had believed.

It wasn't immediately clear, but in the days that followed, the Republicans and the Supreme Court revealed that they were not just inclined but eager to let Donald have his way and, in many cases, enable him. I watched every day as things got worse. Each new transgression landed like a blow. This was America now.

At random moments throughout the days that followed, I thought, How is it possible? How can this have happened? I mean, Jesus Christ, it's Donald. *Donald!* Whenever this reality became conscious, a jolt hit me between the ribs and I felt like I was hallucinating.

But I was screaming into a void. The least worthy, the most vile among us had won—again. He was going to get away with it—again. I could barely move beneath the weight of the unfairness of it all.

When the group moved en masse toward the Treaty Room and the Yellow Oval on the second floor, I hung back. I saw four very young women—aides, judging by the lanyards and IDs they wore around their necks—and approached one who was carrying a clipboard. I asked her if she could get me some Advil.

"Of course," she said. "I'll see what I can do."

She left me to contemplate my other—much worse—problem: How was I going to make it through the rest of this evening without being able to walk? I'd be fine once I got to the dining room, but after dinner we had a very long walk back to the van.

Another woman with a lanyard and ID stood in the middle of the hallway observing the group, now listening to a presentation being given by the White House historian. In her forties, she had an air of authority and was clearly not an aide—she wore an impeccable, expensive suit. I shuffled over to her, looked up (she was at least six inches taller than I was, even without her four-inch stilettos), and steeled myself to ask one of the most absurd questions I'd ever had to ask anybody.

"Excuse me. I know this is a bizarre thing to ask, but I broke my heel on the way in and I'm having a difficult time walking." Given her own choice of footwear, I thought she might be able to empathize with my plight. "Is there any chance there might be a spare pair of shoes lying around that I could borrow?"

She looked down at me from her height. I had offended her. "I don't have any shoes for you." She pivoted and walked briskly off.

The dining room looked very far away.

Following ten years of estrangement that resulted from the lawsuit I brought against my grandfather's estate challenging the will in which he had completely disinherited me, Maryanne and I slowly formed a relationship after my cousin Ivanka's wedding. I can't say we repaired our relationship because, before 2009, we'd never had one. But in an effort, perhaps, to set things right, she and I began to meet for lunch every month or so at a little bistro a couple of blocks from her apartment on the Upper East Side. We chatted, sometimes for hours, about politics, her work as a judge, and, more tentatively, family history.

It was hard to believe this was the same woman I'd known growing up, who, despite my seeing her almost every time I went to the House, rarely spoke to me beyond a clipped greeting. So cool were things between us, even after my father died, that I'd only reached out to her once in all those years. At the time, I was home from Germany—the country from which my great-grandparents had come to America and that I'd chosen in the hopes my grandfather would care, that he might even introduce me to family who still lived not too far from where I would be studying. I'd been there since July 1987 for my junior year abroad from Tufts University and had come back to New York for Christmas, but not because I had any desire to be home. I'd been having a very difficult time in Germany—after five months, my German was not nearly good enough to keep up with the advanced German literature courses I was taking—and instead of staying at Tübingen for the spring semester, I wanted to go back to Tufts instead. I figured it might be easier to make the case in person.

Before coming back, I'd called my mother from a pay phone outside the apartment I shared with four German students, to ask her to find out if I could stay with my grandparents at the House for the week I was back in New York. I hadn't been around cats in over a year, and I was worried I might have an asthma attack if I stayed with her.

When she approached my grandfather about it, he told her that I could not stay with them, despite their four empty bedrooms. If she was worried about my asthma, he said, she should get rid of the cats.

I called Maryanne for advice a few days before Christmas from the phone in my mother's kitchen. I was nervous. I don't think I had ever spoken to her on the phone before, and it had been a year since we'd seen or spoken to each other at all, but I didn't have anybody else in the family to turn to. I was very worried that if I asked my grandfather directly, he'd be even angrier with me than he already seemed to be. Despite my having an aunt and two uncles who had been my trustees since my father died, the family lawyer, Irwin Durben, had been my point person. If I had an unforeseen financial problem or if I needed permission for something, it was Irwin, not anybody in my family, I was supposed to call. But I knew he would tell me I had to stay in Germany. Maryanne seemed the only option.

When she answered the phone, I identified myself as her niece.

"Yes?" she said noncommittally.

I explained my situation: I did not want to go back to Germany, but I wasn't sure how to tell my grandfather.

There was a pause at the other end so long I thought we'd

been disconnected. Finally, I heard her sigh. "Mary," she said, "why are you calling *me*?"

Things had changed since our first lunch in 2009. I had come to look forward to our visits. And then the election happened. Maryanne grew distant in 2020. After November, she became downright dismissive of me, scolding me for my politics and conceding that she had voted for Donald—out of family loyalty.

64

Accepting Maryanne's invitation to the White House was a way for me to extend an olive branch to her, but it had required an extraordinary and psychically damaging degree of compartmentalization and denial to show up, to be cordial, to feel so exposed. Maryanne and I didn't speak again for several months, and I've never spoken to my uncles or Elizabeth or my cousins again.

When I returned from DC, I felt depleted and even less able to stay engaged in my day-to-day life. I barely left the house anymore and eventually was forced to concede that I needed more help than I was getting. My therapist recommended I check into Cottonwood, a treatment center in Tucson, for several weeks of trauma therapy. I agreed to go for three. It was the last thing in the world I wanted to do, but I felt that I didn't have a choice.

The bone-dry desert air flattens space. For the first few days it disoriented me. I misjudged distances and stumbled over imaginary objects. Everything felt two-dimensional and foreshortened. If there had been anyone to reach for, I would have missed my mark by a mile. It took days for me to adjust to the routine, and, with the exception of the therapy groups I had to attend every day, I kept to myself.

Our phones and laptops were kept locked up, and access to them—for one hour in the morning or one hour in the afternoon—was strictly limited to the computer room. I called my daughter, Avary, to check in once a day, but I had no interest in anything else that was going on in the wider world. There was no one else I wanted to talk to.

The only electronic device we were allowed to keep with us was an iPod Shuffle, a one-inch square of metal onto which I had downloaded every song in my library. I kept my earphones in as I walked from one appointment to the next and during meals. I sat alone at a table in the dining hall, defying anybody to come near me.

I clenched my fists and gritted my teeth in a constant state of rage. I fumed at the injustice of having to be there, far away from my daughter. I was plagued by intrusive thoughts, picturing my corpse, wrapped in plastic, being prepared before getting sent back to New York. When I was lucky, I dissociated and surveyed everything with the exquisitely cool detachment of the damned. But mostly, I was angry. I was so fucking angry.

After I'd been there for five days, it was as if a switch had been flipped. I started to talk in groups and asked my fellow patients if I could join them for meals. When I passed a group of people sitting in the lounge chairs outside the nurses' station, instead of averting my eyes and rushing by, I sat with them.

I woke up early and took walks in the desert, steering clear of the small groups of javelinas. At night, a small group of us who were older than the majority of patients, most of whom were in their late teens and early twenties, took the snacks and coffee we'd gotten from the pantry that was open until lights out and brought them to the wrought iron tables and chairs set up next to the lawn. We talked as the moon rose, and the desert hares hopped onto the grass and stretched out in the cool evening air to sleep.

And nobody knew who I was. Nobody knew my last name or my politics or who my family was. It cut both ways, because

I couldn't actually talk about what had landed me there in the first place, but on balance it was a relief.

The new camaraderie made it easier to do the work. I was learning what happens when early traumas aren't confronted and the rifts they create are ignored. And I was beginning to understand how much it had cost me to wait so long to repair them.

In between sessions and groups, we had to do a lot of writing, filling in open-ended statements like:

When I think of sincerely loving myself . . .

I will never give up my self-hatred because if I did, I would have to . . .

I stepped far enough outside of myself to hear—really hear—the cruelty of the language I used against myself, the fluency of my contempt for every aspect of who I had become. I wondered at the audacity of my repeated attempts in the past to *matter*. I recognized with something akin to compassion that if I ever heard another human being speak to Avary the way I spoke to myself, I would murder them with my bare hands.

Although my new friends and fellow patients didn't know my last name or that Donald was my uncle, all of my therapists did. Cammie, my trauma therapist, helped me understand that my reaction to Donald's ascension to the White House was a symptom of the much older trauma.

In order to make any breakthroughs, I was going to have to face the feelings that had become completely detached from my traumatic childhood experiences.

That seemed insane to me. I argued that I had no feelings whatsoever about what my mother had done to me. She countered that that was precisely the problem—the feelings were still there, unacknowledged and unprocessed, but still doing considerable damage, like a sharp shard of glass floating freely beneath my skin. That might be the key to figuring out how to let go of my self-loathing.

Our sessions came to feel like fencing, a series of parries and ripostes that had me reveling in my supreme ability to deflect and pivot. A significant part of me liked the self-loathing because, although I was the target, I was also the one wielding the cruelty. I was hurting myself, but I felt the power in doing it.

Cammie marveled at my skill; she despaired of me. At least that's how I interpreted it.

I started EMDR (eye movement desensitization and reprocessing), during which I focused on a traumatic memory while holding a paddle in each hand that vibrated at different intervals. I picked the most obvious trauma to work on, and every session started with me in the bed next to my mother. My goal was to get out of the room, but after many, many sessions the bed is where I remained. It felt demoralizing that I still had so much further to go even as I understood that it would take more than three weeks to overcome five decades' worth of trauma.

As my stay came to a close, I got nervous. I had no idea what it would be like to be back in the world; I had no idea how I would be able to make it up to Avary; I had no idea how I would handle the isolation of returning to my Republican town, where the number of my friends had been reduced to one.

Even so, I couldn't wait to get home.

65

I lasted two months back home before I had to go back into treatment. I wasn't starting from scratch, but I hadn't laid a glove on the mantra that played constantly in the back of my head: "I don't deserve to be here; I don't deserve to exist."

I planned to stay for five weeks, and I comforted myself with the knowledge that I'd learned a lot during my first three weeks of treatment. I began to realize that I'd been in an almost constant state of grief since the first time my mother put me in bed next to her. Other tragedies and losses became traumas, and I continued to remain disconnected from the grief itself.

Because there was no one to help me make sense of what happened to me, I internalized my own interpretation of what my mother's actions meant. I came to judge myself without mercy. Given all the material advantages I had in my life, I felt deeply ashamed that I hadn't accomplished more.

Facing that was difficult; convincing myself I deserved compassion would be harder, but I committed myself to doing the work. I dug in. I got as close as I could.

Two months earlier, Tucson had been hell, with temperatures approaching 120 and the tarmacs at the Phoenix airport melting. September was gentler; it even rained once or twice. Every morning and evening, I ran in the desert, rich with the smell of honeysuckle, eucalyptus, and animal scat. I hiked up hills, I sprinted. I felt fierce.

When it was time to plan the trip home, I felt ready. I had an agenda: spending more time with Avary and planning more trips with her; going into the city at least once a week; joining a book club or a writer's group; volunteering; and playing tennis again.

I promised to find trauma and EMDR therapists back in New York, and on my final form, "Six reasons I choose to remain in treatment," I wrote:

One: My daughter deserves a mother who is healthy, present, stable, and emotionally available.

Two: I want to contribute more to the world.

Three: I want to know what it's like to live a life that's fulfilling, happy, and productive.

Four: I want to achieve financial and emotional stability.

Five: I want to be free.

Six: I want to live.

Three days before I left for home, I cracked the fifth metatarsal of my left foot and arrived home on crutches.

66

I sat on the couch with my foot elevated for four months. The fracture was so bad, the doctor said I would have been better off if I'd snapped the bone clean in two. The optimism I brought home with me from Tucson lasted a week; my resolve to hang on to what I'd achieved over the course of my eight weeks away lasted two.

And then I received a letter from Sue Craig, the investigative journalist from *The New York Times* who had first come to my house a few months earlier to see if I'd be willing to speak with her about my family's financial history. I'd refused then, but in the interval, she'd written and called several times.

The horrors from the Trump administration continued, from Donald's fascist comments in the wake of the Charlottesville Unite the Right rally and the murder of Heather Heyer to the Department of Justice's overturning of transgender workers' rights, and on and on.

It was no longer clear what I was protecting by not talking to Sue Craig. The family line, as handed down by Maryanne, was that we don't talk to reporters (except Donald, of course). But I wasn't part of the family anymore. And nobody was doing anything to slow Donald down, let alone stop him.

Shortly after Maryanne and I had begun spending time together, I took a break, because every time we met, she brought up the lawsuit I had brought against my grandfather's estate in 1999, which she referred to as "the debacle." She made it clear that she considered herself the injured party and blamed me for ruining the last year of my grandmother's life.

A year or two passed, but then she reached out to me again. I don't know why, but something had shifted, and that's when we started to become genuinely close. But every once in a while, she said something that reminded me of the bargain I was making.

She had told my brother, Fritz, that she planned to give us a gift—the interest on an annuity she had set up years earlier. It was a significant sum, and although I was grateful, I also saw it less as an act of generosity than as her attempt to return a small percentage of the inheritance she and her brothers had stolen from me.

The day had finally arrived. Maryanne answered the door wearing baggy shorts with an FDNY logo on the left leg and a PROPERTY OF THE US ARMY T-shirt that seemed so incongruous I almost laughed. I followed her into the living room and we took our seats by the windows overlooking Central Park and the Metropolitan Museum of Art. With some ceremony she slid a thick envelope toward me. I thanked her, profusely. Stolen inheritance or not, she had no obligation to give me anything.

"My charity," she said, "is almost always anonymous. I can't tell you how gratifying it is to be able to see the impact it has on a recipient of it."

I looked down at the floor, the smile frozen on my face.

I traded my crutches for a cane sometime in January, and, shortly after that, I met with Maryanne again. We didn't go to the bistro anymore but spent my entire visit at her dining room table, which was almost completely covered with stacks of file folders and three-ring binders. On occasion she had a copy of Gwenda Blair's book *The Trumps* nearby with Post-its of various colors sticking out between its pages. Usually at an hour in, regardless of what time I'd arrived, she asked if it was too early for a glass of wine. It turned out it never was.

By then I had handed forty thousand pages of documents over to the *New York Times* reporters and I had done my best, during phone calls and meetings at my house, to give them background information.

And I had learned a few things, too. I saw the copy of my parents' divorce agreement, which essentially guaranteed my mother would never be able to get ahead financially; I read the transcripts of the depositions Maryanne, Donald, and Robert had given (Elizabeth wasn't one of my trustees and hadn't been one of my grandfather's executors, either); and I listened to the recordings of them. Maryanne's voice, in particular, dripped with contempt for us, but they were all devoid of any concern or love or affection for their dead brother or his children.

And I started to have some inkling of just how extraordinarily wealthy my grandfather had been and, in that context, just how mean his treatment of my father had been. I reread my grandparents' wills, which were identical, and remembered the last thing Gam had ever said to me: "You know what your father was worth when he died? A whole lot of nothing."

67

After I graduated from Tufts, I took a year off and worked at a bookstore in Cambridge while I applied to grad schools. When I found out I'd been accepted to Columbia, I moved my stuff back to Jamaica before I left for Europe—I planned to spend the summer in Florence.

My grandmother and I had been essentially estranged since my father died. Since I lived in Somerville, Massachusetts, I only saw her on Thanksgiving and Christmas, and we never spoke on the phone. Since I knew I was moving back to the city in the fall, I intended to make a concerted effort to heal the rift, even though I didn't entirely understand what had caused it.

I flew to London first, intending to visit a friend in Oxford before taking the train south to Italy, but it ended up not working out. I had a week before my lease in Florence started, so I decided to visit Edinburgh instead.

I booked a bed-and-breakfast over the phone, but when I got there, I discovered they allowed their many, many cats to sleep in the guest rooms. By five o'clock the next morning, my inhaler had stopped working, so I left to walk around the city. Edinburgh was one of the most beautiful places I'd ever been, but since I was going to have to change accommodations anyway, I got it into my head that I wanted to visit the Isle of Lewis, my grandmother's birthplace. Some of my father's first cousins still lived there, and I thought it would be a great idea to meet them.

It was a beautiful day in May, and after I bought a map and travel guide at Waterstones, I sat at a table outside trying to figure out my route. I'd have to take the train to Glasgow that evening, stay somewhere near the station, then catch a 5:00 A.M. bus that would take me through the Highlands to the harbor town of Uig, on the Isle of Skye. From Skye I would take the ferry to Tarbert, on the Isle of Harris, which is part of the same landmass as Lewis. Once in Tarbert, I had no idea what I was going to do. I was twenty-two years old and assumed it would all work out. Stornoway wasn't that far from Tarbert—I'd take a cab, then find a hotel in town. I'd call my father's cousin when I got there.

I called my grandmother on a pay phone outside the bookstore and said, "Gam, I'm in Edinburgh. I think I'm going to Stornoway tomorrow morning. Can I have my cousin's phone number?"

It took her a few minutes to get her address book, during which I continued to slide coins into the slot of the pay phone. When she finally came back to give me the number of her niece (another Mary), she suggested I call her before I left Edinburgh. Which I did as soon as she and I hung up. A little boy answered and told me his mom wasn't home.

"I'm your cousin Mary, from New York," I said. "I'm in Edinburgh right now, but I'm taking the ferry to Harris and will be there sometime tomorrow afternoon. I thought I'd come meet all of you."

I asked him to let his mom know I called. He said he would, but I doubted it.

The bus drove through the Highlands under a brilliant blue sky and sunshine that lit up the green of the slowly rolling hills. The landscape and the sky were stunning, but by the time the bus pulled into the ferry terminal, the sky had darkened and rain poured down in torrents. I had two hours to kill, so I sat in the waiting room smoking cigarettes and writing postcards while rain lashed against the windows.

The wind picked up during the crossing. It was my favorite

kind of weather for a boat trip, wild and stormy, and it reminded me of the trips to Nantucket we took when I was a kid. As soon as the ferry docked at the harbor, however, the sun came out again. A surprising number of people jammed the tourist office, and I waited in line to find out how best to get to Stornoway. I noticed a woman looking at me. She walked over and said, "Are you Mary?" It was my cousin, who had somehow deciphered the message I'd left with her son and figured out which ferry I'd be on.

Her two brothers, William and Alistair, were waiting in a car out front. During the drive, Nana, as Mary was called, invited me to stay with her and her two kids—her husband was away working on an oil rig in the North Sea.

I spent most of the time with Nana. We played Scrabble with the kids, and I listened to her talk on the phone in Gaelic while she fixed lunch or dinner. She walked with me to the harbor and showed me around Stornoway. It was impossible to picture my stoic, indoor grandmother as a child of these moors and peat bogs and craggy shores, exposed to these punishing elements and vast skies. I could not imagine her being moved in any way by the indescribable beauty of it.

We passed the small airport, and I thought of the black-and-white photograph on the table in the library. Gam stood at the top of the plane stairs with her fox-fur stole around her shoulders, looking less like a returning daughter than a visiting dignitary.

My grandmother's nephew Callum invited me to have dinner with him and his wife one evening. They were relaxed and easy to get along with. Everybody called him Cim because, as a child, he'd gotten hold of a Magic Marker and written his initials all over the walls of his bedroom—CIM for Callum Ian MacLeod.

William and Alistair, bachelors who lived across the street in my grandmother's childhood home, drove me around the island and took me to the beach the day before I left. The sand was as white as any I'd seen, and the Minch—the forty-mile stretch of water between Lewis and the mainland—looked almost inviting, even though it couldn't have been more than fifty degrees outside and the water was even colder.

On my last day there, Nana walked me to the ferry in Stornoway that would take me to Ullapool. I'd spend the night in Inverness, and from there begin my journey south to Florence.

I'd only been there for three days, but they already felt more like family to me than my own aunts and uncles. Even so, I never saw them again.

68

In January 2018, I joined the *New York Times* team for a tour of my grandfather's empire. We visited Trump buildings I'd never even heard of. After eight hours of driving around Queens and Brooklyn, there were still more than a dozen we hadn't seen.

After that, whenever I showed up at the building on Fifth Avenue for what I'd come to call day-drinking with Maryanne, I activated my phone's voice memo recorder as soon as I sat down across from her. She never noticed.

Maryanne had finally decided to sell her house in Palm Beach.

"When Grandpa died," she told me, "I finally had some money, so I bought a little cottage."

Her "cottage" was on the market for twenty-four million dollars, but because of its proximity to Mar-a-Lago, Donald was interested in buying it from her.

"First, he tried to get me to take papers [give him a loan directly without his having to go to a bank to get a mortgage], and I laughed in his face. Well, he had to try." She smiled. "Now he's trying to Jew me down."

When the hell is she going to ask me if it's time for a glass of wine? I thought.

69

When Sue Craig and Russ Buettner published their massive piece in *The New York Times* on October 2, 2018, I realized that the calculus involved in damaging Donald, in making a dent in the hold he had over the Republican Party, had only gotten more difficult since 2016. Death by a thousand lashes became my mantra.

Because the *Times* opus did not reveal a single event but, rather, detailed a lifelong pattern of fraud, misrepresentation, and possible criminality, I thought it would do more than make a dent. The piece also put to rest, once and for all (or at least it should have), the myth that Donald was self-made, legitimate, or successful. Yet we watched in amazement as Donald got away with transgressions against women, veterans, and basic human decency so frequently that I got sick of hearing the phrase, "This would have ended the career of any other politician."

As proud as I was to have been even a small part of the *Times* investigation, I needed to do more. And I needed to do it publicly.

The publication of *Too Much and Never Enough* in July 2020 changed everything and nothing. I had been a very private person for my entire life, and now I was supposed to know how to juggle requests for interviews, fundraisers, and endorsements. I was expected to be media savvy. People asked me to send emails to a network I didn't have. Although the number of my Twitter followers went from ninety to hundreds of thousands overnight, I knew very few people in the real world.

People I'd admired for most of my life sent me emails and

DMs and actual letters, but I didn't know how to respond; responding, in fact, felt presumptuous.

I had finished the book while I was quarantining in my basement in April 2020, and COVID was still surging that summer. Everything was done via Zoom.

And then there were the lawsuits, my family's love language. My uncles, Donald and Robert, had sued to prevent the publication of my book. When that failed, they sued to prevent me from speaking about it. In the fall of 2020, I brought a fraud suit against Donald, Robert, and Maryanne as the executors of my grandfather's estate, based on information from the *New York Times* investigation that in turn had been based on the discovery documents I'd given them.

I'd seen Rob once since Ivanka's wedding, in 2009, during which he made a show of saying, "I think the statute of limitations on family conflict has passed." He repeated that phrase several times in a gregarious way that would have convinced anybody who didn't know him not just that he was a good guy but that he meant what he said. He did not.

This became clear when Fritz and I, a few months after the wedding, were summoned to Maryanne's apartment, presumably to address "the elephant in the room," as she put it. Robert stayed for an hour and then opted not to join us for lunch. The next time I saw him was nine years later, in the lobby of the hotel in DC, waiting for our ride to the White House.

Rob had thoroughly revealed himself after the election— sucking up to a brother he had hated for decades, spouting Fox propaganda, and espousing white evangelical hatred. Maryanne told me about his bursts of irrational rage toward her and his bizarre sycophancy toward Donald. But in his speech at the dining room table in the residential dining room, he outdid himself. As he droned on, referring to his older brother as "Mr. President" at every turn, my contempt for him grew. It didn't surprise me when he agreed, at Donald and Maryanne's insistence, to take the lead in the lawsuit against me despite the fact that he had recently been in the ICU of Mount Sinai Hospital. He died two months later.

When my brother and I sued my grandfather's estate in 1999, after months of trying to negotiate with my uncle Robert to reach a fair settlement, Maryanne came up with the idea of canceling the health insurance we'd been receiving through my grandfather's company since we were born. She believed this would be an effective way to get us to drop our lawsuit because my infant nephew was gravely ill, and taking away our insurance would have been potentially catastrophic to my nephew's health and my brother's solvency. Donald supported this plan because, as he said, "Why should we give him medical coverage? They sued my father, essentially. I'm not thrilled when someone sues my father."

We weren't suing my grandfather—he was dead after years of decline due to Alzheimer's disease, and unlikely to be affected by the lawsuit—and before his death lawyers had warned him that the draconian nature of our disinheritance would likely end in litigation. But by then, Donald had been bullying weaker parties into submission for years, getting his way not because he had the better claim or the better case, but because he could outspend his adversaries and he had no sense of basic human decency to hold him back.

My brother and I had to initiate another lawsuit to force Maryanne, Donald, and Robert to reinstate my nephew's health insurance. This was another massive expense and provided my aunt and uncles with yet another outlet for their cruelty. Their lawyer, a nasty piece of work who acted like a thug every step of the way, referred to the round-the-clock nurses—who had been hired because my brother's son William was still having seizures that sometimes caused his heart to stop—as overpriced babysitters. He went on to suggest my brother and sister-in-law learn CPR if they were so concerned.

The only people I heard discuss my family's strategic cruelty before the 2016 election were MSNBC's Lawrence O'Donnell and David Cay Johnston of DCReport, for which I was deeply grateful. But nobody else noticed that the Republican candidate for the presidency had willfully endangered the life of a sick infant. There was too much else to be horrified by, after all. And far too many of Donald's supporters simply didn't care.

Then there was an ironic aftermath. A few months after we settled the lawsuit, my then-partner and I found out we were having a baby. I was the happiest I'd ever been, until the day my daughter was born. But when my brother heard the news, he stopped speaking to me. He wouldn't answer my emails or phone calls. He didn't even respond to me after the September 11 attacks, when I tried frantically to get in touch with him to make sure he hadn't been in the city that day.

I finally heard from him two weeks after Avary was born. He emailed me to say that we were not welcome at his house for Thanksgiving, where we'd been celebrating it for years. He did not approve of my life choices, he wrote matter-of-factly. And that was it.

We did end up going to Thanksgiving that year because my sister-in-law told me the invitation was still open, but my brother ignored me and barely acknowledged my daughter's existence. This went on for eight years. We reconciled in 2009, but too much damage had been done, and it didn't last. When I told him in 2019 that I was writing a book about the family, which was slated to be published in advance of the election, he stopped speaking to me again. By the time *Too Much and Never Enough* was released, in July 2020, we were completely estranged.

By September, when the clamor over the book had passed, I focused entirely on the election. I was concerned, deeply, but I didn't feel the same kind of dread I'd felt in 2016—not because I was more confident, but because we were living through so many contemporaneous tragedies that it was impossible to stay constantly attuned to the potential for even more catastrophe and still function. I kept myself cocooned, head down, blinders on.

Even during the delay after Election Day, while we waited for the votes to be counted and Donald declared premature victory, I felt hopeful if not optimistic. This wait felt much less onerous than the weekslong delay after the 2000 election.

Then Biden won. We were going to be OK.

70

Almost every day for months, I've found myself trying to find the thread. How did I get here? How is it, once again, that I find myself stuck on the couch, trapped in my apartment, isolated and feeling as though I haven't got a friend in the world?

Getting to the origin of this paralysis became an obsession. I no longer believed it was a problem I could solve, but rather a pattern I had to disrupt. But first, I needed to know—was there a precise moment or a specific triggering event?

The world around me had changed—warped by COVID and Donald's continued presence in our politics. But I was different, too, fundamentally altered by my asthma, the torture, the medication, the weird prominence of my family, the incompatibility of the family's vast wealth and my own sense of impoverishment, my father's alcoholism, and everything I had witnessed.

All of it had marked me. Always, there had been an invisible but impenetrable veil floating between me and every person I wanted to be close to. The distance between what might have been and how things actually were continued to widen. I started to look forward to doing TV interviews because it was the only time I felt engaged. But as soon as I closed the laptop, it was as if a switch was flipped, and I became the expressionless, affectless person who sat on the couch most of the day scrolling through Twitter.

That's who I should be, I sometimes thought. That's who I was. It wasn't a performance; I had become so detached from that person, though. In the Before Times, which for me ended on November 8, 2016, I felt like myself, and in the right company, I felt at ease, confident, and comfortable in my own skin.

It had gotten to the point where I only felt like that person—somebody who could speak in complete paragraphs with nuance and a command of the facts—when I was talking to another person in a faraway studio whom I couldn't even see.

My opportunities for connection were greater than they'd ever been, but the more isolated I felt, the more theoretical they seemed. I watched as my friends lived their lives, while other friends slid away from me, or I from them, sometimes for a legitimate reason, good or bad, sometimes for no reason at all. In my darkest moments, I lost my faith in friendship almost completely.

To be a public person whose private people had no idea what I was going through was incredibly lonely.

The truth, a truth, is that I was a happy kid, but as I adjusted in order to survive, I became warped to the contours of the circumstances of growing up.

Even so, each time I experienced a setback, I got back on my feet and then tried to accomplish more. But there was attrition. Each time, it got harder; there was less to draw on, a peeling away of strength and purity of intent. Extrinsic motives intruded, and the dark places in between got darker and encroached further. Sometimes it felt like I was a chicken who'd had her head cut off, but it just took a very long time for me to realize it. How many chances do you get, right?

If history rhymes, so does trauma. And although I had often stood on the brink of facing my trauma down, I had never completed the work. Was it bravery I needed? No, I needed to be out in the world again. I needed to allow myself to have that privilege again. But wouldn't that take some measure of courage? I took merciless inventory. No, it wasn't courage I needed. It was love. And I had none of that to give myself. I had no grace to extend.

My love for other people so often felt like an expression of self-loathing, and my self-loathing didn't just damage, it annihilated. When I felt thwarted or incompetent or stupid, I spoke to myself with such violence that it hollowed me out. I knew what I was doing, and I could have controlled it if I wanted to, but I felt a certain devious satisfaction in my ability to be so cruel to myself.

What kept me inside was no longer simply fear but a shame so deep it forced me to withdraw from the world, because I finally understood that there was no way I could ever prove I deserved my place on this planet.

And then my mother called.

71

I'm scared," her message said. She'd been to see an oncologist. She had cancer and would be needing surgery. She wanted me to accompany her to her doctor's appointments.

That simple declarative sentence, "I'm scared," gave me a small chill at the nape of my neck. I'm not the kind of person who easily turns away from somebody in pain, from somebody who's afraid. But I didn't feel anything when I listened to her message, other than the chill, and I didn't call her back.

My mother and I hadn't seen each other since June 2019, and we hadn't spoken since October 2020. At first, there was nothing intentional about our falling out of touch, but over time, I realized I preferred it that way, and her increasingly infrequent attempts to contact me went unanswered.

Under these circumstances, though, I didn't think I had a choice. Still, I put off calling her. There's a difference between having no feelings about something and not being able to feel, and I worried that if I spoke to her again, she would manage to find, with the expertise of a surgeon wielding an exquisitely sharp scalpel, the one nerve only she could expose.

I had been in graduate school the last time I had given her the chance.

It was the end of my last year at the Derner Institute of Advanced Psychological Studies at Adelphi University. I was in my late thirties, Avary was four, and my class was preparing for our fourth-year skits, which always started with a slideshow. If we wanted to be included, we had to submit pictures of ourselves as a baby or a kid in elementary or middle school, plus one of our own children and spouses, if we had them.

I didn't have any old pictures of myself, so I asked my mother if she could find some for me. I was very specific: no professional or studio portraits; no dresses or skirts; nobody else in the picture with me; and, if possible, I wanted to be doing something I liked, like playing sports or driving a boat.

My mother agreed to look. When she called to tell me she'd found a few photographs that might work, she offered to meet on campus and hand-deliver them.

It was one of those stunning late spring days in New York, and I waited outside the building for her. When she pulled up, I walked over to the car and she passed me a manila envelope through the passenger-side window.

I thanked her and waved as she drove away. I sat on one of the benches by the entrance and sorted through what she had brought me.

The first was a studio portrait of me with my brother. I must've been fourteen, because my hair was feathered and I wore a cross around my neck. I was wearing a peach turtleneck and a rust-colored blazer and looked like an idiot.

The next was another professional photograph that had been taken in Ohio. Fritz and I sat on a split-rail fence, a pasture in the background. Picture after picture showed me posed sitting next to my brother, in a formal setting, in a dress, or otherwise looking completely unlike myself.

There were two smaller pictures at the bottom of the envelope. In the first, I was walking down the street, wearing jeans and a red jacket and carrying a tennis racket. I must have been about eight and I was on my way to the basketball courts a few blocks from the Highlander, just off 164th Street. I was pretty far away from whoever was taking the picture, and my hair, long and windblown, was covering most of my face.

When I turned over the second, I froze. In it, I was sitting at the round table near the kitchen still wearing my school uniform. It looked like I was doing my homework. I was holding a pen. My left elbow was on the table and my head rested in my hand. I seemed tired and my hair was uncombed. I looked, unsmiling, at the camera. I couldn't fathom why anyone would take the picture, let alone keep it. I couldn't imagine what my mother was thinking when she put it in the manila envelope.

A semester earlier, I had taught a course on trauma and discussed with my students the case of Hedda Nussbaum, who had been brutally and repeatedly beaten by Joel Steinberg over the course of several years. Steinberg had murdered their adopted daughter, Lisa, whom he had also horribly abused. In the course of my research, I came across the last picture that had ever been taken of Lisa as she sat in her first-grade classroom on Halloween. She's unkempt, her hair in knots, and she looks beyond hope. In the first split second I saw that photograph, I thought it was me, even though she and my six-year-old self looked very little alike.

I felt like somebody had punched me in the solar plexus. My eyes stung with tears, and I thought, She literally can't help but hurt me.

I'd never let her hurt me again.

72

I spoke to my mother briefly before her surgery, then again just before the rehab facility was ready to discharge her. Both times, she talked as if we'd never lost touch. She complained that she didn't know what I was doing, but she didn't ask, and I had no interest in telling her.

I engaged the home health aide she requested. A few days after she got home, she called again to make sure I had arranged for somebody to run her errands and clean her house. With every word she spoke, I got angrier.

She had a hearing aid, so I spoke loudly and distinctly, but she kept interrupting me. This happened several times. Finally, I stopped speaking.

"Hang on," she said. "Let me check something." When she got back on the phone, she told me that her hearing aid was working fine. "I guess it just can't hear you," she said. I went cold.

I'd spent enough of my life thinking I was going to suffocate to death with her lying next to me doing nothing. I couldn't feel fear—either hers or mine—anymore. Just incandescent rage.

73

I was standing in the kitchen of my apartment on Cape Cod when my phone rang. It was Lachlan Cartwright, a reporter for the *Daily Beast* who had scooped the imminent publication of my first book despite the immense efforts of dozens of people over the course of more than a year and a half to keep it secret. I'd since gotten over it—he did great reporting, which had had the ancillary and unintentional benefit of helping the book by getting the word out ahead of time—but I couldn't imagine why he'd be calling me at nine o'clock at night.

I'd spent the afternoon at the beach kayaking, so my guard was down. When I answered, Lachlan immediately asked me how I felt about Donald's new lawsuit. I had no idea what he was talking about. He clarified: "Your uncle is suing you and *The New York Times* for a hundred million dollars for breach of contract. I wanted to know what you think."

What I wasn't thinking was that I was on the record, so I said, "I think he's a fucking loser."

Donald filed his lawsuit a year after I filed *my* lawsuit against him, Maryanne, and my uncle Robert's estate for fraud and breach of fiduciary duty. In the ensuing three years, very little has happened. As of January 2024, *The New York Times* has been removed as a defendant, but he's still suing me for a hundred million dollars.

It's an odd thought that brings me full circle. While Donald had a hand in destroying his older brother, and triumphed over that, he knows—*he knows*—that nothing can change the fact that Freddy was superior to him in every way. He can pretend all he wants that he was smarter or more successful or that the qualities that made Freddy so much the better man didn't count for anything, just as he can pretend that he's more popular than Taylor Swift. But Donald Trump—he knows.

My grandfather disinherited me (in his will he singled me out as "the issue of Frederick C. Trump, Jr."). With a significant assist from Donald and Maryanne, he took my father away from me. Then Maryanne, Donald, and Robert stole the inheritance that would have come to me from my father—and they did it while they were my trustees (and my aunt and uncles). Yet it's still not enough.

I kept losing and he kept winning against me. This meant that I had less of a platform from which to challenge him. As time went on and the cases against him piled up, the only one that was never mentioned anymore was mine. More than that, it underscored that my family's crimes against my father and me, and by extension my daughter, didn't matter. And not only were they deemed inconsequential—the judge having found that the fraud used to coerce me into signing a document was of less consequence than my having signed the document—it wasn't enough. Because Donald's case against me was succeeding. If the crime was foundational, so, too, was the impunity that followed it.

74

I don't know what I expected after the 2020 election, but it wasn't this. Sometimes I think, I don't want to do this anymore. None of us does. We're all worn out, depleted; the divisions have become chasms, which often feel as though they're etched in marble. Once again, we're on the brink of losing democracy while constantly fighting a rear guard action against fascism, and keeping informed has begun to feel like a constant IV drip of poison being injected directly into our bloodstream. It's corrosive.

And yet . . .

Four years after E. Jean Carroll first brought her defamation suit against Donald Trump, she prevailed, to the tune of $88.3 million. My lawsuits may be stalled; three of the four criminal trials may not be brought before the election; but E. Jean demonstrated a level of courage and integrity that reduced Donald to the petty, vengeful sexual abuser that he is. And she did this simply by showing and telling the truth.

This is not how I ever imagined I'd be measuring my life, but here we are, Donald and I, still on diametrically opposite ends of everything, just as we were at my grandparents' formal dining room table.

The difference now—he's not the only one with power.

The Good in Us

And as the gods are strange, and punish us for what
is good and humane in us as much as for what is
evil and perverse, I must accept the fact that one is
punished for the good as well as for the evil that one
does.

—OSCAR WILDE, *De Profundis*

I took the elevator to the sixth floor, the highest floor of Sunnyside Towers. The dimly lit hallway still smelled of stale cigarette smoke, as it had when my father lived there half a century ago; the carpets were the same seal grey, slick with age and lack of care. I walked to the end of the hallway where Dad's apartment had been. In 1973, he owned 15 percent of this building, yet my grandfather had granted him dispensation to live there as if it were an act of charity.

I had already visited Sunnyside Towers in January 2018 with Sue Craig and Russ Buettner, as part of a tour of my grandfather's Brooklyn and Queens real estate empire. We'd only seen the outside of the building, which had been jarring enough. It had the same boxy redbrick exterior as Fred Trump's other buildings, but without the trappings of extravagant landscaping or a dramatic entryway. I'd forgotten the building had a pool, which made me feel a little hollow.

This time I was determined to get inside. I slipped in with a

UPS delivery man; there was no doorman to notice my trespass. The lobby hadn't changed in the intervening years: the planters on either side of the entryway stairs were filled with plastic ferns and philodendrons that looked as if they hadn't been dusted since Dad lived there.

I'd set out that warm, sunny summer morning to re-create the trip the *New York Times* reporters and I had taken. While I visited some of the same buildings—as well as some we didn't manage to see during our eight-hour journey through Queens and Brooklyn, because there were simply too many of them—I also took a trip to the All Faiths Cemetery in Middle Village, Queens. My great-grandparents and grandparents were buried there along with my father's ashes.

Like many cemeteries in Queens, All Faiths is enormous. I had only been there twice: in 1981, on the day of my father's funeral, and in 1999, the day my grandfather was buried there. There was no way I would be able to find my way to the plot through the maze of paths, so I stopped by the office to get directions.

I said to the man behind the counter, "I'm here to visit the grave of Mary Trump," which was an odd thing to hear myself say.

He didn't hesitate. "I'll get the number for you. Just give me a minute." He crossed to a bookshelf at the back of the room and pulled a thick black binder down. After setting it on a desk, he leafed through its pages, and then he went through them again. He consulted with a colleague and then, with a puzzled look on his face, walked back to the counter and said, "That page seems to be missing."

"Really?" I asked. Suddenly, this felt like a bad idea and I didn't want to be there. I'd come back some other time. I almost told him not to bother, but before I could, he said he'd check in the back.

A few minutes later he returned with a photocopy of the missing page and, without explanation, uncapped a yellow highlighter and traced the route to my family's grave site.

"Once you get to this road"—he pointed to a location on the map—"the headstone will be six rows in. Mr. Trump," he said, not specifying which one, although it was almost certainly Robert, the uncle who did the best job of pretending to be human, "had a sidewalk installed about ten years ago."

I got back in my car, crossed over Metropolitan Avenue, and drove through the cemetery entrance. The road, more of a trail really, took a sharp left turn, ran parallel to Metropolitan for a while, then jogged around a Denny's that jutted into a corner of the cemetery.

There were deep potholes, and as I concentrated on trying to avoid them, I almost missed the scenery: the cemetery looked like it had been desecrated. Tombstones were knocked over and tree limbs littered the grounds. The weeds were so overgrown, I drove right past the "sidewalk" Mr. Trump had installed. It was a narrow path of cracked cement and overgrown grass. Nothing looked familiar.

When I finally found my family's headstone, the only thing that distinguished it from its immediate neighbors was its extreme whiteness. Everything else seemed wrong: my father's dates— October 14, 1938–September 26, 1981 (how was it possible that I was almost thirteen years older than he'd been when he died?)— the grounds, neglected and overgrown, the graves crowded together. When my grandfather insisted that my father's ashes be buried here more than forty years earlier, not one of my aunts or uncles had objected. At the time, I thought it was because they wanted a place to visit. It looked as if nobody had been there since the sidewalk was installed. It looked as if nobody in my family had ever been there at all.

Someone, almost certainly a stranger, had planted a couple of plastic American flags in the soil in front of the headstone. They were filthy and torn. I pulled them out of the ground and threw them in the trunk of my car.

Then I drove to Sunnyside.

For the two years my father lived in that dank, dingy apartment, he had been almost completely isolated. He had no job then, and my brother and I stopped visiting him because it had begun to feel dangerous with his drinking and erratic moods. Then, somehow, he had gathered himself and moved to Florida, determined to start over. In the end, I don't know if he could have managed to pull it off, but he got so sick he never had a chance to find out. Back in New York, back in the House, he survived his open-heart surgery. And he still had hope, otherwise he wouldn't have written that letter to the FAA, with a two-hundred-dollar check enclosed, requesting to renew his pilot's license. But he couldn't survive his father.

The malign forces arrayed against him were external. In the end, his thin frame couldn't possibly support the weight of his family's pathologies and my grandfather's contempt. "[H]e actually lived a long time longer than you would expect," Donald said of his forty-two-year-old brother in an interview. He claimed Freddy's fatal flaw was that he gave himself to other people.

There was no joy in the family my father grew up in besides the joy he himself possessed, which existed in abundance. He clung to it as long as he could, even as my grandfather took away his cars and his boats and his planes and then finally the only thing he had left—his sense of possibility.

A few weeks ago, New York City was plunged into a brutal cold snap, with winds so strong the wind chill barely rose above zero. It snowed for the first time in two years, and my cat chased the snowflakes as they fell outside the window, as she had as a kitten the last time it snowed.

After a few days, the wind died down and I went out to run some errands, the only reason in the last few months I ever left my apartment. I'm usually out for only fifteen or twenty minutes. Much longer than that and my chest starts to tighten and I need to go home.

One of my errands took longer than I wanted it to, and by the time I started walking toward my building, the sun was beginning to set. The temperature was dropping, but I kept walking west, down Canal Street, across the West Side Highway, until I was walking south along the Hudson River.

I breathed the cold air in, but I didn't feel cold. By the time I got to the esplanade near Warren Street, the sky was on fire. The beauty of it knocked me back. I was surprised I could still feel that sense of wonder. I sat by the edge of the river until the sun had dropped below the horizon and the last of the evening light had died. The lights of the city—my city—shone behind me. There's no way to know if a chance for redemption or even forgiveness exists anymore, but in that moment, I felt the world opening up again.

I leaned my head back, breathed deeply, and took it all in.

ABOUT THE AUTHOR

Avary L. Trump

Mary L. Trump is the author of the international #1 bestseller *Too Much and Never Enough: How My Family Created the World's Most Dangerous Man* and the *New York Times* bestseller *The Reckoning: Our Nation's Trauma and Finding a Way to Heal*. She holds a PhD from the Derner Institute of Advanced Psychological Studies at Adelphi University. She writes the newsletter *The Good in Us* and is the host of *The Mary Trump Show* on YouTube.